ONDORI

A DOLL-MAKER'S TREASURY

Designed by **KYOKO YONEYAMA**

Contents

★Copyright © 1985 ONDORISHA PUBLISHERS, LTD. All rights reserved.
★Published by ONDORISHA PUBLISHERS, LTD., 32 Nishigoken-cho, Shinjuku-ku, Tokyo 162, Japan.
★Sole Overseas Distributor: Japan Publications Trading Co., Ltd.
  P.O. Box 5030 Tokyo International, Tokyo, Japan.
★Distributed in the United States by Kodansha International / USA Ltd.
  through Harper & Row, Publishers, Inc., 10 East 53rd Street, New York, New York 10022.
  Australia by Bookwise International, 1 Jeanes Street, Beverley, South Australia 5009, Australia.

10 9 8 7 6 5 4 3 2 1

ISBN 0-87040-653-1
Printed in Japan

*S*weet *Sixteen*

Instructions on page 81.

Debutantes

D   C

Instructions on page 84.

B　A

3

Friends

Instructions on page 88.

*B*onneted Girls

Instructions on page 92.

Country Girl

Instructions on page 96.

Cute Memo Holders

C

E

Instructions on page 100.

A

B

D

LITTLE GREY
RABBIT

Helpful Kiddies

Instructions on page 104.

A

C

Mascots

Instructions on page 16.

C

B

D

E

A

15

Mascots, shown on pages 14 & 15.

MATERIALS FOR ONE DOLL:
For face: See page 69. For hood and body: Quilted fabric, 25 cm square; cotton print, 25 cm by 13 cm; lace edging, 1.5 cm by 20 cm; one piece of ready-made appliqué. For hair: 3-ply yarn; ribbon, 0.6 cm by 40 cm.
FINISHED SIZE: 15 cm tall.

DIRECTIONS:
Make face following instructions on pages 69–73. Cut 2 pieces for body, adding 1 cm all around for seam allowance. With right sides facing, sew 2 pieces together, leaving neck and bottom open for turning. Trim extra seam allowance. Turn inside out. Attach head to body securely. Attach hair, make features, and put hood on.

Actual-size patterns

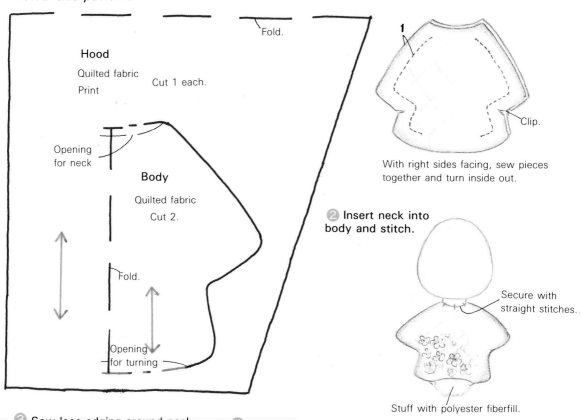

Hood
Quilted fabric
Print
Cut 1 each.

Fold.

Opening for neck

Body
Quilted fabric
Cut 2.

Fold.

Opening for turning

1 Sew 2 pieces of body together.

1

Clip.

With right sides facing, sew pieces together and turn inside out.

2 Insert neck into body and stitch.

Secure with straight stitches..

Stuff with polyester fiberfill.

3 Sew lace edging around neck.

Run gathering stitches along edge of 20 cm lace edging, place around neck and pull up thread.

1.5

Overcast opening closed.

4 Attach hair to head.
(Use 3-ply yarn.)

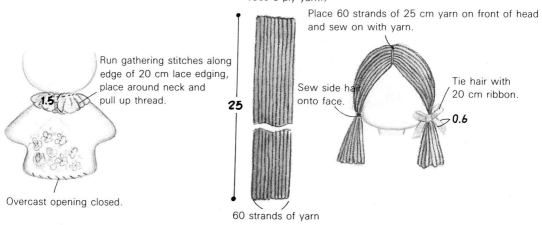

Place 60 strands of 25 cm yarn on front of head and sew on with yarn.

Sew side hair onto face.

Tie hair with 20 cm ribbon.

25

0.6

60 strands of yarn

⑤ **Sew hood.**

Fold.

Sew back seam.

With right sides facing,
sew quilted fabric and lining together,
leaving opening for turning.
Turn inside out.

15

A:

Turn up top edge.

Nose

Eye 0.7

0.3 0.4

Glue nose and eyes in place.

Rub rouge.

Embroider mouth.

Glue appliqué onto body.

Back

Apply glue inside of hood and place hood on head.

B:

Eye 0.2

0.4

Sew side hair onto face.

Run gathering stitches along edges of 2 lace edgings, place them around neck and pull up thread.

Glue appliqué onto body.

Tie hair with ribbon.

C:

Place hair on head and take a long stitch at left.

Glue appliqué onto body.

D:

Glue appliqué onto body.

Hair (3-ply yarn)

25

Sew hair onto face.

70 strands of yarn

E:

Sew center of hair onto head.

Trim bangs.

60 strands of yarn

40 strands of yarn

40 strands of yarn

Tie hair with 20 cm ribbon.

Glue hair onto head.

Glue appliqué onto body.

17

Grandma and Twin Granddaughters

Instructions on page 20.

Grandma and Twin Granddaughters,

shown on pages 18 & 19.

MATERIALS:

For face: See page 69.

[For Grandma] For dress: Quilted fabric, 75 cm by 40 cm; felt, 6 cm square; braid, 0.6 cm by 152 cm; one piece of ready-made appliqué; cardboard, 12 cm by 6 cm. For apron: Cotton broadcloth, 27 cm by 20 cm; cotton lace edging, 2 cm by 85 cm; ribbon, 1.1 cm by 76 cm. For hair: Cotton glove. Light pink heavy-duty sewing thread, #30. Polyester fiberfill.

[For Twins] For dress: Quilted fabric, 22 cm by 12 cm; lace edging, 1.5 cm by 33 cm; cotton broadcloth, 8 cm by 7 cm; ribbon, 0.6 cm by 40 cm and 0.4 cm by 30 cm;

braid, 0.7 cm by 44 cm. For hair: One sock.

FINISHED SIZE: Grandma, 38 cm tall. Twins, each 14.5 cm tall.

DIRECTIONS:

Make face following instructions on pages 69–73. For Grandma: Glue nose onto face. Embroider wrinkles with light pink heavy-duty sewing thread. Sew hair onto head. Sew bodice and sew skirt onto bodice. Sew bottom of skirt. For Twins: Follow illustrated instructions on next page.

Actual-size patterns are shown on page 109.

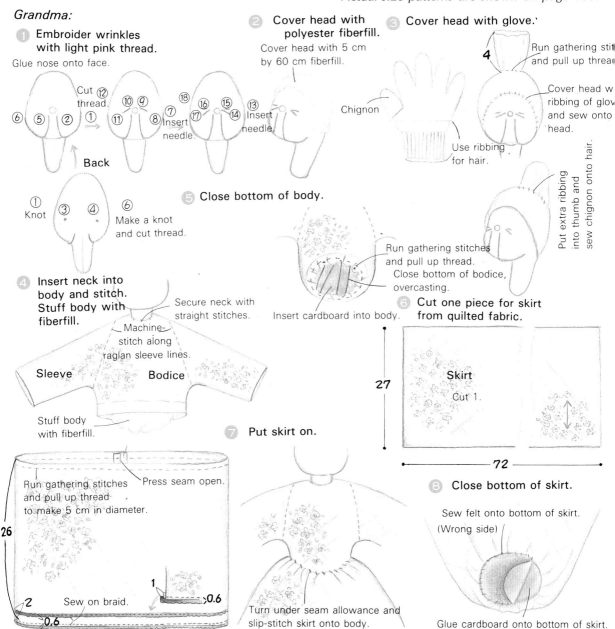

Grandma:

1 Embroider wrinkles with light pink thread.

Glue nose onto face.

2 Cover head with polyester fiberfill.

Cover head with 5 cm by 60 cm fiberfill.

3 Cover head with glove.

Run gathering stitches and pull up thread.

Chignon

Use ribbing for hair.

Cover head with ribbing of glove and sew onto head.

Put extra ribbing into thumb and sew chignon onto hair.

Back

Knot

Make a knot and cut thread.

4 Insert neck into body and stitch. Stuff body with fiberfill.

Secure neck with straight stitches.

Machine-stitch along raglan sleeve lines.

Sleeve   Bodice

Stuff body with fiberfill.

5 Close bottom of body.

Run gathering stitches and pull up thread.

Close bottom of bodice, overcasting.

Insert cardboard into body.

6 Cut one piece for skirt from quilted fabric.

27

Skirt
Cut 1.

72

7 Put skirt on.

Turn under seam allowance and slip-stitch skirt onto body.

8 Close bottom of skirt.

Sew felt onto bottom of skirt.
(Wrong side)

Glue cardboard onto bottom of skirt.

Run gathering stitches and pull up thread to make 5 cm in diameter.

Press seam open.

26

2   Sew on braid.   0.6

1

0.6

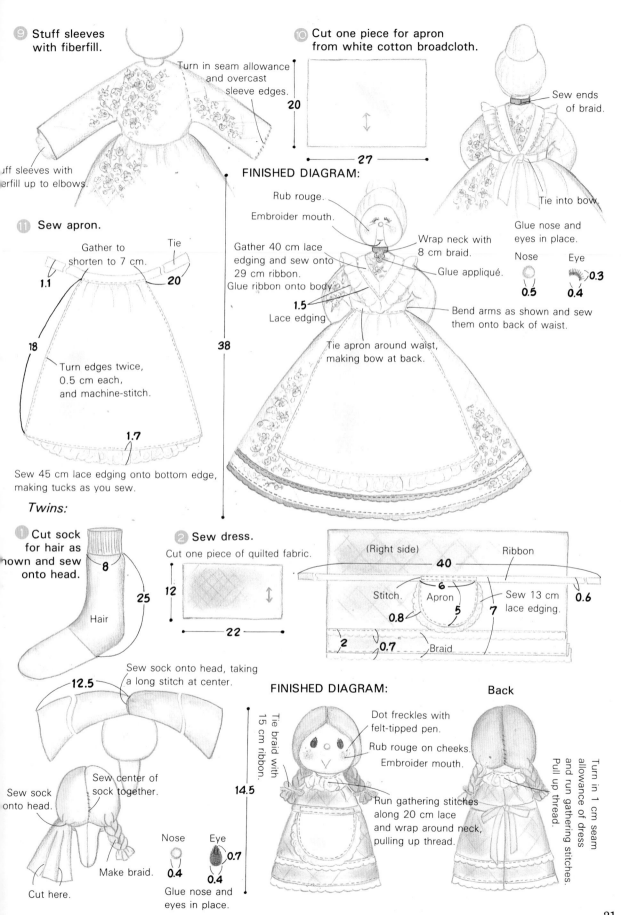

⑨ Stuff sleeves with fiberfill.

Turn in seam allowance and overcast sleeve edges.

20

Stuff sleeves with fiberfill up to elbows.

⑩ Cut one piece for apron from white cotton broadcloth.

27

FINISHED DIAGRAM:

Rub rouge.

Embroider mouth.

Gather 40 cm lace edging and sew onto 29 cm ribbon. Glue ribbon onto body.

1.5

Lace edging

Wrap neck with 8 cm braid.

Glue appliqué.

Tie apron around waist, making bow at back.

Bend arms as shown and sew them onto back of waist.

Sew ends of braid.

Tie into bow.

Glue nose and eyes in place.

Nose   Eye

0.5   0.4   0.3

⑪ Sew apron.

Gather to shorten to 7 cm.   Tie

1.1   20

18

38

Turn edges twice, 0.5 cm each, and machine-stitch.

1.7

Sew 45 cm lace edging onto bottom edge, making tucks as you sew.

Twins:

① Cut sock for hair as shown and sew onto head.

8

25

Hair

② Sew dress.

Cut one piece of quilted fabric.

12

22

(Right side)   Ribbon

40

Stitch.   Apron   Sew 13 cm lace edging.

0.8   5   7   0.6

6

2   0.7   Braid

FINISHED DIAGRAM: Back

Sew sock onto head, taking a long stitch at center.

12.5

Sew center of sock together.

Sew sock onto head.

Make braid.

Cut here.

Nose   Eye

0.4   0.7

0.4

Glue nose and eyes in place.

Tie braid with 15 cm ribbon.

14.5

Dot freckles with felt-tipped pen.

Rub rouge on cheeks.

Embroider mouth.

Run gathering stitches along 20 cm lace and wrap around neck, pulling up thread.

Turn in 1 cm seam allowance of dress and run gathering stitches. Pull up thread.

*B*ottle Friends

Instructions on page 24.

Bottle Friends, shown on pages 22 & 23.

MATERIALS:
For face: See page 69. For body: Felt, 28 cm by 10 cm;
Tyrolean tape, 1.2 cm by 30 cm; cardboard, 6 cm square.
For hair: Mohair yarn.
FINISHED SIZE: 11 cm tall.

DIRECTIONS:
Make face following instructions on pages 69–73. Make
body with felt. Insert head into body and glue. Stuff body
with fiberfill, covering poking area of neck. Sew bottom
onto body. Sew hair onto head and make features.

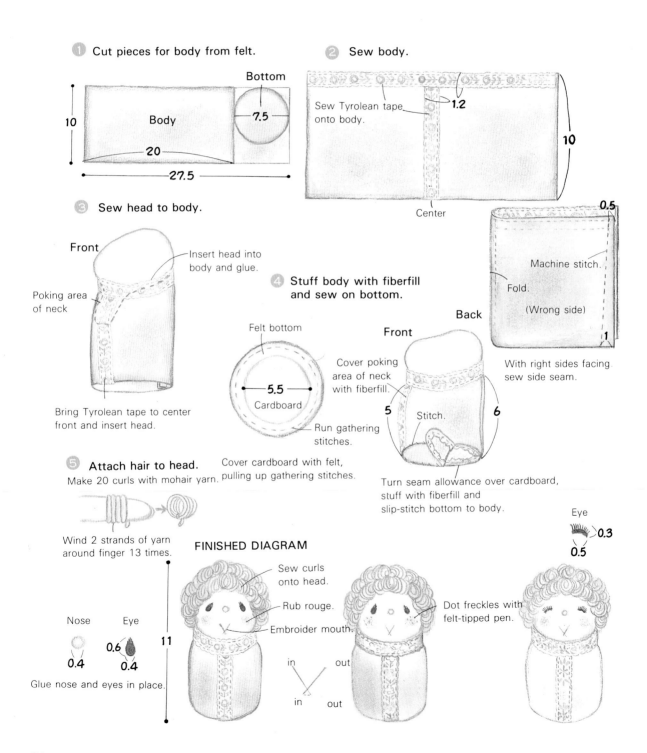

① Cut pieces for body from felt.

Bottom

Body

10   7.5

20

27.5

② Sew body.

Sew Tyrolean tape onto body.   1.2

Center   10

0.5

Machine stitch.

Fold.

(Wrong side)

1

③ Sew head to body.

Front

Insert head into body and glue.

Poking area of neck

Bring Tyrolean tape to center front and insert head.

④ Stuff body with fiberfill and sew on bottom.

Felt bottom

5.5

Cardboard

Run gathering stitches.

Cover cardboard with felt, pulling up gathering stitches.

Cover poking area of neck with fiberfill.

Back

Front

With right sides facing, sew side seam.

5   Stitch.   6

Turn seam allowance over cardboard, stuff with fiberfill and slip-stitch bottom to body.

⑤ Attach hair to head.
Make 20 curls with mohair yarn.

Wind 2 strands of yarn around finger 13 times.

Eye

0.3

0.5

FINISHED DIAGRAM

Sew curls onto head.

Rub rouge.

Embroider mouth.

Dot freckles with felt-tipped pen.

Nose   Eye

0.4   0.6   0.4

Glue nose and eyes in place.

11

in   out

in   out

See reference on page 65 as possible solution.

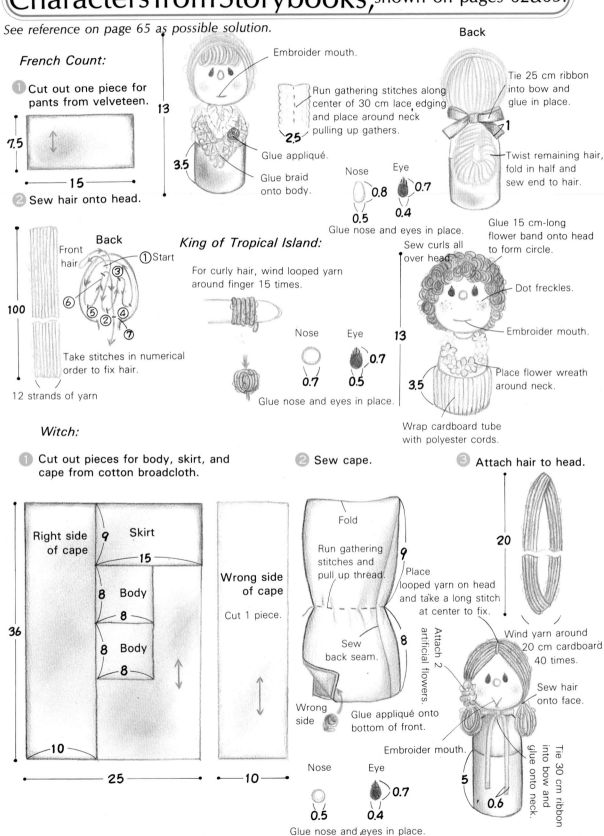

French Count:

1 Cut out one piece for pants from velveteen.

7.5

15

2 Sew hair onto head.

13

Embroider mouth.

3.5

2.5

Run gathering stitches along center of 30 cm lace edging and place around neck pulling up gathers.

Glue appliqué.

Glue braid onto body.

Back

Tie 25 cm ribbon into bow and glue in place.

1

Twist remaining hair, fold in half and sew end to hair.

Nose

0.8

0.5

Eye

0.7

0.4

Glue nose and eyes in place.

Front hair

Back

100

① Start

③

⑥

⑤ ② ④

⑦

Take stitches in numerical order to fix hair.

12 strands of yarn

King of Tropical Island:

For curly hair, wind looped yarn around finger 15 times.

Nose

0.7

Eye

0.7

0.5

13

Glue nose and eyes in place.

Glue 15 cm-long flower band onto head to form circle.

Sew curls all over head.

Dot freckles.

Embroider mouth.

3.5

Place flower wreath around neck.

Wrap cardboard tube with polyester cords.

Witch:

1 Cut out pieces for body, skirt, and cape from cotton broadcloth.

2 Sew cape.

3 Attach hair to head.

Right side of cape

9

Skirt

15

8 Body

8

8 Body

8

36

10

25

Wrong side of cape

Cut 1 piece.

10

Fold

Run gathering stitches and pull up thread.

9

Place looped yarn on head and take a long stitch at center to fix.

8

Sew back seam.

Attach 2 artificial flowers.

Wrong side

Glue appliqué onto bottom of front.

Embroider mouth.

Nose

0.5

Eye

0.7

0.4

Glue nose and eyes in place.

20

Wind yarn around 20 cm cardboard 40 times.

Sew hair onto face.

5

0.6

Tie 30 cm ribbon into bow and glue onto neck.

Three Sisters (Pajama Bags)

Instructions on page 28.

Three Sisters, shown on pages 26 & 27.

MATERIALS:
For face: See page 69.
[For Khaki-dressed Doll] Quilted fabric, 54 cm by 34 cm; 12 cm-wide lace edging, 50 cm; 4 cm-wide lace edging in shades of khaki – 108 cm each for (a), (b), (c) and (d); 54 cm for (e); 162 cm for (f); 3 cm-wide lace edging, 84 cm for (g); 23 cm zipper; mohair yarn.
[For Cream-dressed Doll] Quilted fabric, 46 cm by 37 cm; lace edging, 5 cm by 200 cm for (a), 3.5 cm by 184 cm for (b), 4 cm by 260 cm for (c); ribbon, 1.8 cm by 80 cm and 0.6 cm by 56 cm; 20 cm zipper; baby yarn.
[For White-dressed Doll] Quilted fabric, 40 cm by 30 cm; cotton broadcloth, 60 cm by 30 cm; lace edging, 3 cm by 160 cm for (a), 4.5 cm by 210 cm for (b), 60 cm by 80 cm for (c), 1.5 cm by 30 cm; ribbon, 1 cm by 70 cm and 0.6 cm by 40 cm; 18 cm zipper; mohair yarn.

FINISHED SIZE: Khaki-dressed doll, 39 cm tall. Cream-dressed doll, 43 cm tall. White-dressed doll, 37 cm tall.
DIRECTIONS:
Make face following instructions on pages 69–73. For Khaki-dressed doll: Sew 13 pieces of lace edging onto quilted fabric, overlapping lace as shown. Fold in half with right sides facing and sew side seam to make tube. Attach head to body. Run gathering stitches around top of skirt and pull up thread. Attach hair to head. Put on hat and make features. For cream-dressed and white-dressed dolls: Make as for khaki-dressed doll.
If you cannot find the right color lace edging, dye white lace.

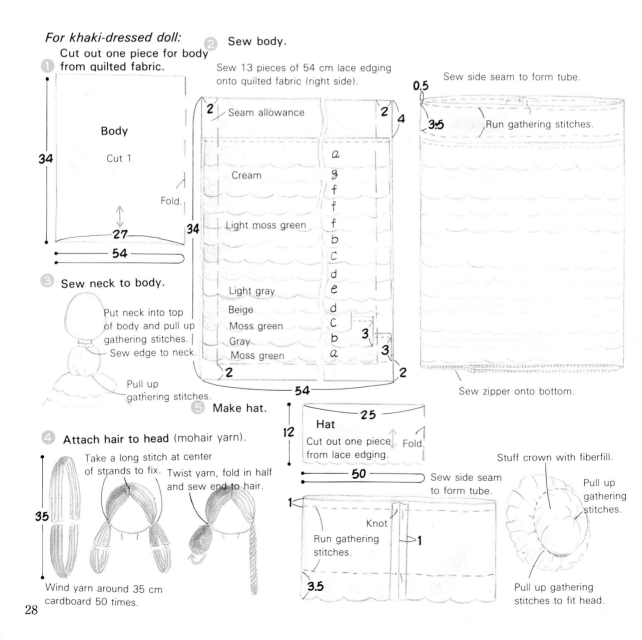

For khaki-dressed doll:
① Cut out one piece for body from quilted fabric.

Body
Cut 1

34
27
54
Fold.

② Sew body.
Sew 13 pieces of 54 cm lace edging onto quilted fabric (right side).

2   Seam allowance   2   4
Cream   a
                             g
                             f
                             f
Light moss green   f
                             b
                             c
                             d
                             e
Light gray   e
Beige   d
Moss green   d
Gray   c
Moss green   b
                             a
34
2   54   2
3   3

Sew side seam to form tube.
0.5
3.5   Run gathering stitches.

Sew zipper onto bottom.

③ Sew neck to body.
Put neck into top of body and pull up gathering stitches.
Sew edge to neck.
Pull up gathering stitches.

④ Attach hair to head (mohair yarn).
Take a long stitch at center of strands to fix.
Twist yarn, fold in half and sew end to hair.
35
Wind yarn around 35 cm cardboard 50 times.

⑤ Make hat.
12
Hat
Cut out one piece from lace edging.
25
Fold.

50
Sew side seam to form tube.
1
Knot
1
Run gathering stitches.
3.5

Stuff crown with fiberfill.
Pull up gathering stitches.
Pull up gathering stitches to fit head.

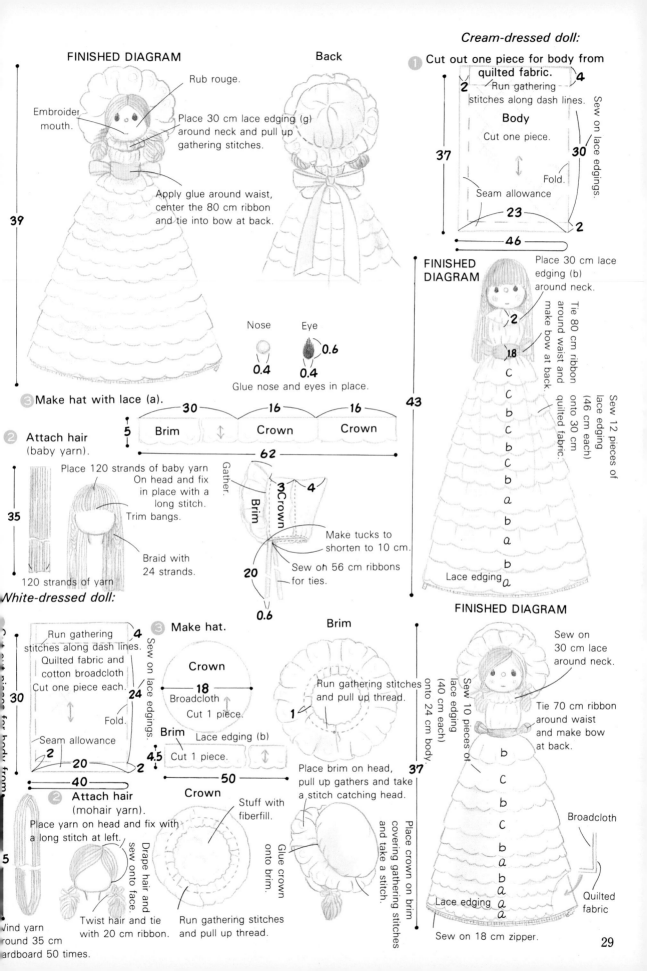

FINISHED DIAGRAM

Embroider mouth.

Rub rouge.

Place 30 cm lace edging (g) around neck and pull up gathering stitches.

Apply glue around waist, center the 80 cm ribbon and tie into bow at back.

39

Back

Nose

0.4

Eye

0.6

0.4

Glue nose and eyes in place.

③ Make hat with lace (a).

30   16   16

5   Brim   Crown   Crown

62

② Attach hair (baby yarn).

Place 120 strands of baby yarn On head and fix in place with a long stitch. Trim bangs.

35

Braid with 24 strands.

120 strands of yarn

Gather.

3 Crown 4

Brim

Make tucks to shorten to 10 cm.

Sew on 56 cm ribbons for ties.

20

0.6

Cream-dressed doll:

① Cut out one piece for body from quilted fabric.

Run gathering stitches along dash lines.

Sew on lace edgings.

2   4

37

Body

Cut one piece.

30

Fold.

Seam allowance

23

2

46

FINISHED DIAGRAM

Place 30 cm lace edging (b) around neck.

Tie 80 cm ribbon around waist and make bow at back.

2

18

Sew 12 pieces of lace edging (46 cm each) onto 30 cm quilted fabric.

43

c
c
b
c
b
c
b
a
b
a
b

Lace edging a

White-dressed doll:

Run gathering stitches along dash lines. Quilted fabric and cotton broadcloth Cut one piece each.

4

Sew on lace edgings.

30   24

Fold.

Seam allowance

2   20   2

40

② Attach hair (mohair yarn).

Place yarn on head and fix with a long stitch at left.

5

Drape hair and sew onto face.

Twist hair and tie with 20 cm ribbon.

Wind yarn round 35 cm ardboard 50 times.

③ Make hat.

Crown

18

Broadcloth ↑ Cut 1 piece.

Brim

4.5 Lace edging (b) Cut 1 piece.

Crown

Stuff with fiberfill.

Glue crown onto brim.

Run gathering stitches and pull up thread.

Brim

Run gathering stitches and pull up thread.

1

Place brim on head, pull up gathers and take a stitch catching head.

50

Place crown on brim covering gathering stitches and take a stitch.

FINISHED DIAGRAM

Sew on 30 cm lace around neck.

Tie 70 cm ribbon around waist and make bow at back.

Sew 10 pieces of lace edging (40 cm each) onto 24 cm body.

37

b
c
b
c
b
a
b
a
a

Lace edging a

Broadcloth

Quilted fabric

Sew on 18 cm zipper.

C*lowns*

Instructions on page 32.

A

B

C

Clowns, shown on pages 30 & 31.

MATERIALS:
For face: See page 69.
[For each clown] For body and hands: White rayon, 30 cm by 18 cm. For hands: White cotton jersey, 20 cm by 7 cm. For edgings of hat and outfit: Lace edging, 3 cm by 220 cm; braid, 1 cm by 85 cm. For shoes: Felt, 18 cm by 10 cm. For hair: 4-ply yarn. For stuffing: Wood-wool; polyester fiberfill.
[For A (right)] Cotton print, 90 cm by 60 cm.
[For B (center)] Cotton print, 90 cm by 65 cm.
[For C (left)] Cotton print, 90 cm by 70 cm.

FINISHED SIZE: 44 cm tall.
DIRECTIONS:
Make face following instructions on pages 69–73. Stuff body firmly with wood-wool and hands with fiberfill to make flat hands. Sew top and pants. Sew shoes at bottom of pants and hands at sleeve edges. Sew top and pants onto body. Attach hair, make features and sew on hat.

See pages 108 and 109 for actual-size patterns.

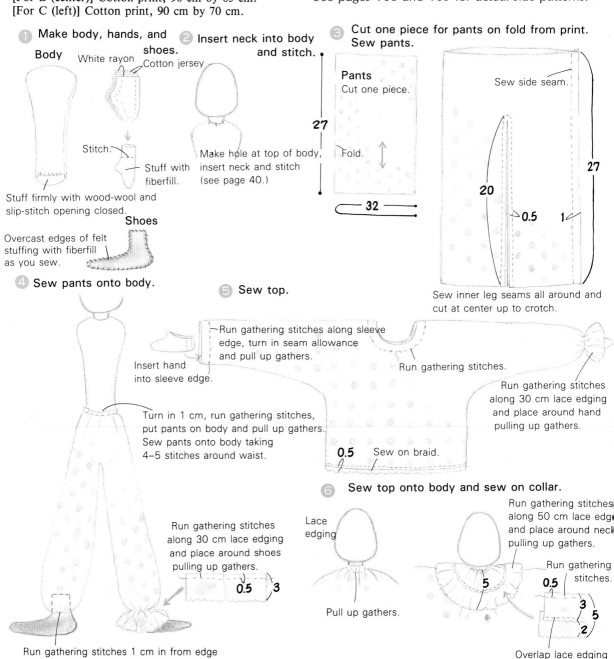

1 Make body, hands, and shoes.

Body
White rayon
Cotton jersey

Stitch.
Stuff with fiberfill.

Stuff firmly with wood-wool and slip-stitch opening closed.

Shoes
Overcast edges of felt stuffing with fiberfill as you sew.

2 Insert neck into body and stitch.

Make hole at top of body, insert neck and stitch (see page 40.)

3 Cut one piece for pants on fold from print. Sew pants.

Pants
Cut one piece.

27

Fold.

32

Sew side seam.

20
27
0.5   1

Sew inner leg seams all around and cut at center up to crotch.

4 Sew pants onto body.

Insert hand into sleeve edge.

Turn in 1 cm, run gathering stitches, put pants on body and pull up gathers. Sew pants onto body taking 4–5 stitches around waist.

Run gathering stitches along 30 cm lace edging and place around shoes pulling up gathers.
0.5   3

Run gathering stitches 1 cm in from edge and turn in seam allowance.
Insert shoes into pants and pull up gathers.

5 Sew top.

Run gathering stitches along sleeve edge, turn in seam allowance and pull up gathers.

Run gathering stitches.

Run gathering stitches along 30 cm lace edging and place around hand pulling up gathers.

0.5   Sew on braid.

6 Sew top onto body and sew on collar.

Lace edging

Pull up gathers.

Run gathering stitches along 50 cm lace edging and place around neck pulling up gathers.

Run gathering stitches.

5
0.5
3
5
2

Overlap lace edging and stitch.

7 Sew hat.

8 Attach hair (4-ply yarn).

Sew center back seam.

0.5 Sew on braid.

20

60 strands of yarn

Place 60 strands of yarn on top of head and take a long stitch at center.

Trim bangs.

Nose

Eye

0.5

0.6
0.4

Glue nose and eyes in place.

44

A:

Glue hat onto head.

Rub rouge.

Embroider mouth.

B:

Nose

Eye

0.8

0.7
0.5

Glue nose and eyes in place.

Embroider mouth.

Rub rouge.

Run gathering stitches.

0.5

3

2

5

Lace edging

Overlap lace edging and stitch.

C:

Nose

Eye

0.6

0.7
0.5

Glue nose and eyes in place.

Rub rouge.

Embroider mouth.

City Girls

Instructions on page 36.

City Girls, shown on pages 34 & 35.

MATERIALS:

For face: See page 69.

[For each doll] For body, arms, and legs: White rayon, 60 cm by 35 cm. For arms: Apricot pink cotton jersey, 20 cm by 25 cm. For legs: White cotton jersey, 30 cm by 35 cm. For drawers and petticoat: White cotton broadcloth, 46 cm by 17 cm; white lace edging, 2.5 cm by 24 cm. For shoes: Felt, 15 cm by 10 cm. For hair: Mohair yarn. For stuffing: Wood wool; cotton and polyester fiberfill. Cardboard.

[For Doll with Checked Dress] Gingham checks, 69 cm by 30 cm; cotton lace edging, 3.5 cm by 14 cm; ribbon, 0.6 cm by 112 cm.

[For Doll with Floral Dress] Floral print, 67 cm by 30 cm; cotton lace edging, 4 cm by 84 cm; ribbon, 0.6 cm by 50 cm; 2 buttons, 0.7 cm in diameter; cotton yarn.

FINISHED SIZE: 53 cm tall.

DIRECTIONS:

Make face following instructions on pages 69–73. Use Country Girl pattern on page 96 for body, arms, and legs. Make body and put dress on following illustrated instructions. Make features and attach hair.

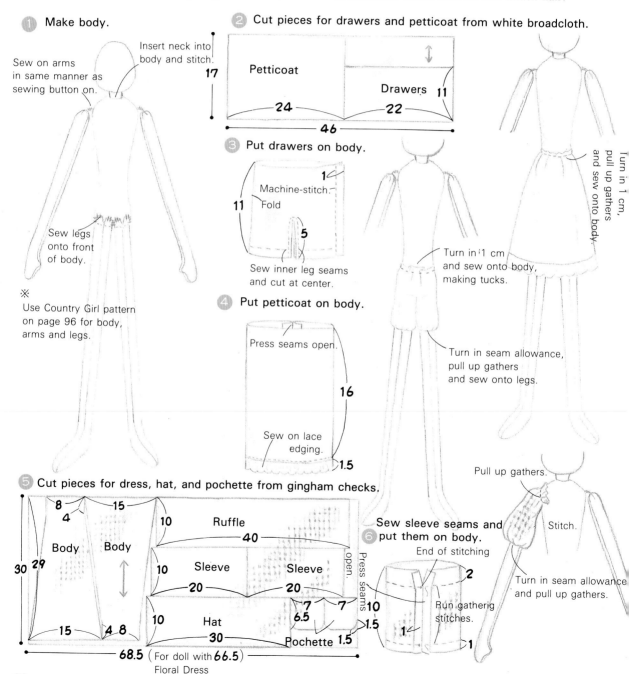

1 Make body.

Sew on arms in same manner as sewing button on.

Insert neck into body and stitch. 17

Sew legs onto front of body.

※ Use Country Girl pattern on page 96 for body, arms and legs.

2 Cut pieces for drawers and petticoat from white broadcloth.

Petticoat 24
Drawers 22 11
46

3 Put drawers on body.

1
Machine-stitch.
11 Fold
5
Sew inner leg seams and cut at center.

4 Put petticoat on body.

Press seams open.
16
Sew on lace edging. 1.5

Turn in 1 cm, pull up gathers and sew onto body.

Turn in 1 cm and sew onto body, making tucks.

Turn in seam allowance, pull up gathers and sew onto legs.

Pull up gathers. Stitch.

Turn in seam allowance and pull up gathers.

5 Cut pieces for dress, hat, and pochette from gingham checks.

8 15
4
Body Body
30 29
15 4 8

10 Ruffle 40
10 Sleeve 20 Sleeve 20
10 Hat 30
7 7
6.5
Pochette 1.5

open.
Press seams open. 10 1.5

68.5 (For doll with 66.5) Floral Dress

6 Sew sleeve seams and put them on body.

End of stitching 2
Run gathering stitches. 1
1

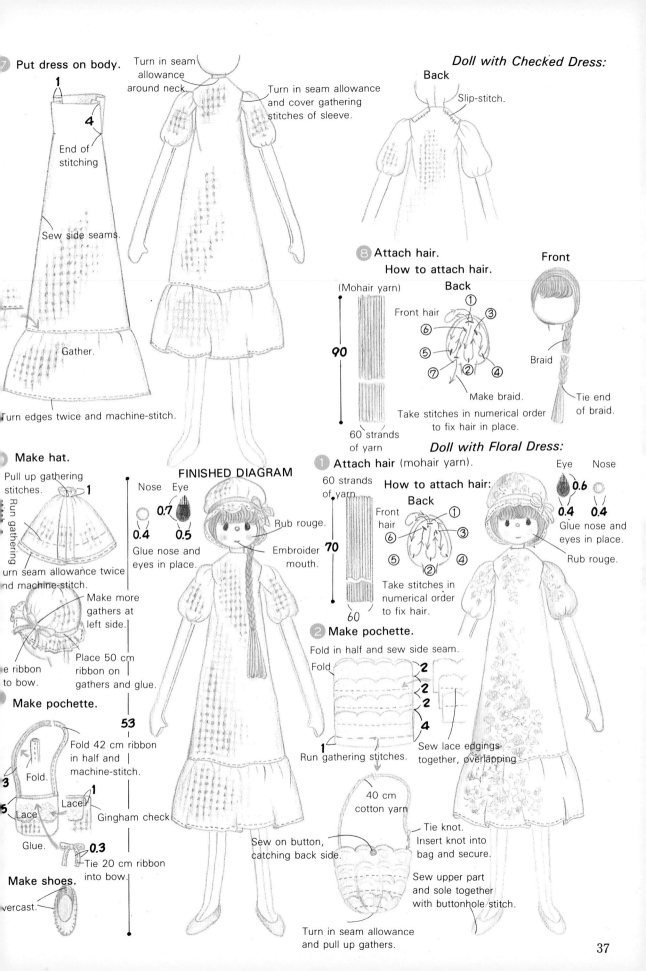

7 Put dress on body.

End of stitching

Sew side seams.

Gather.

Turn edges twice and machine-stitch.

Turn in seam allowance around neck.

Turn in seam allowance and cover gathering stitches of sleeve.

Doll with Checked Dress:

Back

Slip-stitch.

8 Attach hair.

How to attach hair.

(Mohair yarn)

90

60 strands of yarn

Back

Front hair

Make braid.

Take stitches in numerical order to fix hair in place.

Front

Braid

Tie end of braid.

Doll with Floral Dress:

1 Attach hair (mohair yarn).

60 strands of yarn

70

60

How to attach hair:

Back

Front hair

Take stitches in numerical order to fix hair.

Eye 0.6

Nose

0.4   0.4

Glue nose and eyes in place.

Rub rouge.

Make hat.

Pull up gathering stitches.

Run gathering

Turn seam allowance twice and machine-stitch.

Make more gathers at left side.

Place 50 cm ribbon on gathers and glue.

tie ribbon to bow.

Make pochette.

Fold 42 cm ribbon in half and machine-stitch.

3   Fold.

5   Lace

Lace

Lace

Glue.

Gingham check

0.3

Tie 20 cm ribbon into bow.

Make shoes.

Overcast.

FINISHED DIAGRAM

Nose   Eye

0.7

0.4   0.5

Glue nose and eyes in place.

Rub rouge.

Embroider mouth.

53

Gingham check

2 Make pochette.

Fold in half and sew side seam.

Fold

2
2
2
4

1

Run gathering stitches.

Sew lace edgings together, overlapping

40 cm cotton yarn

Tie knot. Insert knot into bag and secure.

Sew upper part and sole together with buttonhole stitch.

Sew on button, catching back side.

Turn in seam allowance and pull up gathers.

37

Raindrops

Instructions on page 40.

Raindrops, shown on pages 38 & 39.

MATERIALS:
For face: See page 69. For body, arms, and legs: White rayon, 60 cm by 9 cm. For arms and legs: Cotton jersey, 44 cm by 9 cm. For hat and dress: Cotton print, 44 cm by 20 cm; lace edging, 1 cm by 22 cm; lace edging with lamé thread, 3.5 cm by 50 cm. For hair: Pearl cotton #5. For stuffing: Wood-wool, cotton, and polyester fiberfill; wire, #16.

FINISHED SIZE: 18 cm tall.
DIRECTIONS:
Make face following instructions on pages 69–73. Stuff body firmly with wood-wool, hands and feet with fiberfill, arms and legs with rolled-up cotton. For flexible arms and legs, don't roll cotton too tight. Sew head, arms and legs onto body. Sew on dress.

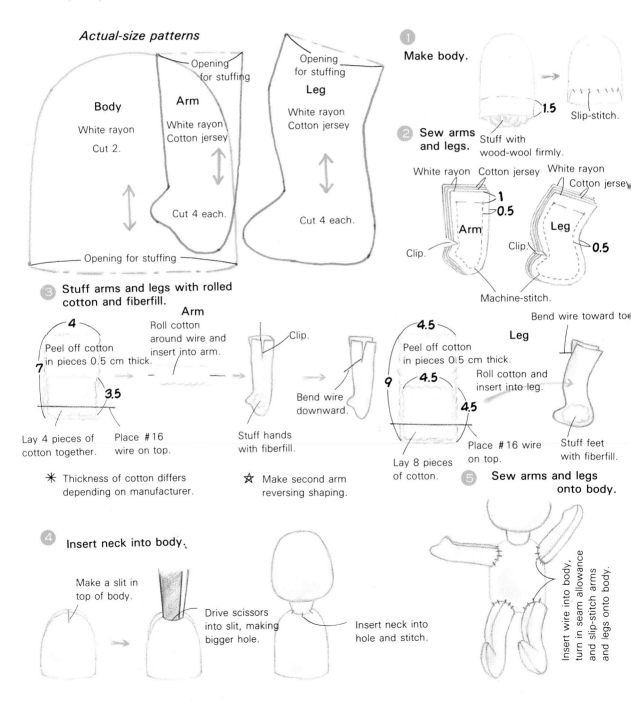

Actual-size patterns

Body
White rayon
Cut 2.

Opening for stuffing

Arm
White rayon
Cotton jersey
Cut 4 each.

Opening for stuffing

Opening for stuffing

Leg
White rayon
Cotton jersey
Cut 4 each.

① Make body.
1.5
Slip-stitch.

② Sew arms and legs. Stuff with wood-wool firmly.

White rayon   Cotton jersey   White rayon   Cotton jersey
1
0.5
Arm
Clip.

Leg
0.5
Clip.
0.5
Machine-stitch.

③ Stuff arms and legs with rolled cotton and fiberfill.

Arm
4
Peel off cotton in pieces 0.5 cm thick.
Roll cotton around wire and insert into arm.
7
3.5
Lay 4 pieces of cotton together.   Place #16 wire on top.

Clip.
Bend wire downward.
Stuff hands with fiberfill.

* Thickness of cotton differs depending on manufacturer.

☆ Make second arm reversing shaping.

Leg
4.5
Peel off cotton in pieces 0.5 cm thick.
4.5
9
4.5
Lay 8 pieces of cotton.   Place #16 wire on top.
Roll cotton and insert into leg.
Bend wire toward toe
Stuff feet with fiberfill.

⑤ Sew arms and legs onto body.

④ Insert neck into body.
Make a slit in top of body.
Drive scissors into slit, making bigger hole.
Insert neck into hole and stitch.

Insert wire into body, turn in seam allowance and slip-stitch arms and legs onto body.

⑥ Cut pieces for pants, top, and hat from cotton print.

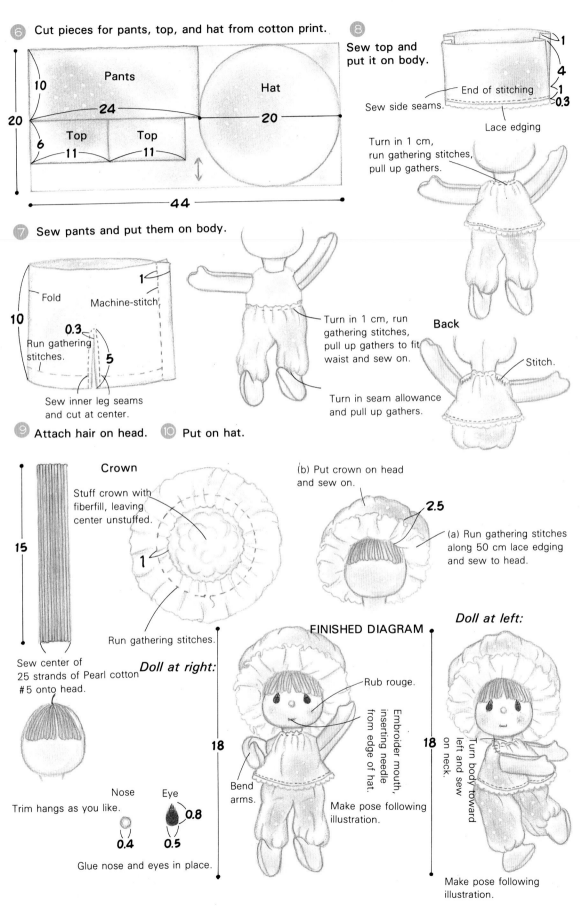

Pants

10

20

24

6 Top 11 Top 11

Hat

20

44

⑧ Sew top and put it on body.

1

4

1

0.3

End of stitching

Sew side seams.

Lace edging

Turn in 1 cm, run gathering stitches, pull up gathers.

Back

Stitch.

⑦ Sew pants and put them on body.

Fold

Machine-stitch.

1

10

0.3

5

Run gathering stitches.

Sew inner leg seams and cut at center.

Turn in 1 cm, run gathering stitches, pull up gathers to fit waist and sew on.

Turn in seam allowance and pull up gathers.

⑨ Attach hair on head. ⑩ Put on hat.

Crown

Stuff crown with fiberfill, leaving center unstuffed.

15

1

Run gathering stitches.

Sew center of 25 strands of Pearl cotton #5 onto head.

Nose

Trim hangs as you like.

0.4

Eye

0.8

0.5

Glue nose and eyes in place.

(b) Put crown on head and sew on.

2.5

(a) Run gathering stitches along 50 cm lace edging and sew to head.

FINISHED DIAGRAM

Doll at left:

Doll at right:

Rub rouge.

Embroider mouth, inserting needle from edge of hat.

18

Bend arms.

Make pose following illustration.

18

Turn body toward left and sew on neck.

Make pose following illustration.

41

Babies of Dandelion

42

Instructions on page 44.

43

Babies of Dandelion, shown on pages 42 & 43.

MATERIALS:
For face: See page 69. For hands: White rayon and cotton jersey, 10 cm square each. For body: Terry cloth, 50 cm by 18 cm; felt, 7 cm square; thick cardboard, 7 cm square; weight; polyester fiberfill. For hair: 4-ply yarn.

FINISHED SIZE: 20 cm tall.

DIRECTIONS:
Make face following instructions on pages 69–73. Use thick cardboard for bottom so that baby can stand. Put weight at bottom. Make babies following illustrated instructions. Make features and poses following illustration or as you desire.

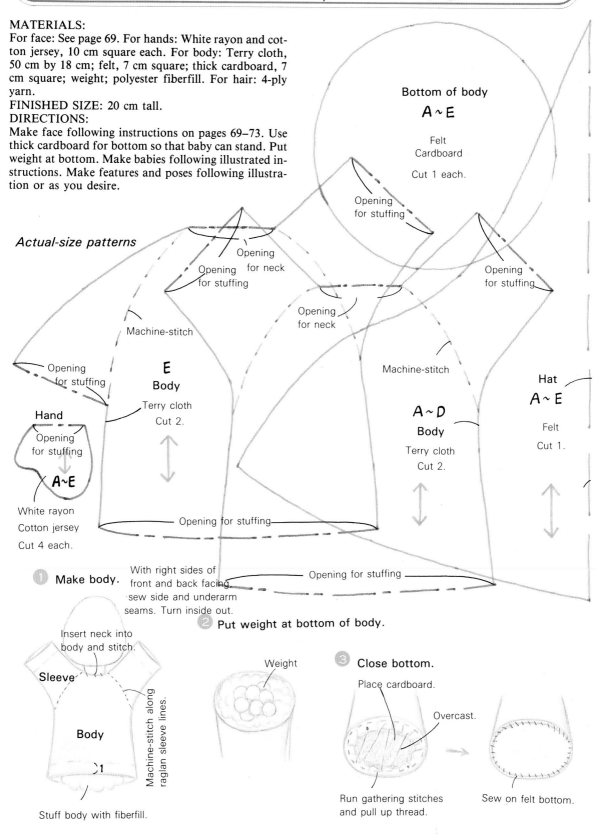

Actual-size patterns

Bottom of body
A ~ E
Felt
Cardboard
Cut 1 each.

Opening for stuffing

Opening for neck

Opening for stuffing

Opening for neck

Opening for stuffing

Machine-stitch

Opening for stuffing

E
Body
Terry cloth
Cut 2.

Machine-stitch

Hand
Opening for stuffing

A ~ E

White rayon
Cotton jersey
Cut 4 each.

A ~ D
Body
Terry cloth
Cut 2.

Hat
A ~ E
Felt
Cut 1.

Opening for stuffing

Opening for stuffing

① **Make body.** With right sides of front and back facing, sew side and underarm seams. Turn inside out.

Insert neck into body and stitch.

Sleeve

Machine-stitch along raglan sleeve lines.

Body

⊃1

Stuff body with fiberfill.

② **Put weight at bottom of body.**

Weight

③ **Close bottom.**

Place cardboard.

Overcast.

Run gathering stitches and pull up thread.

Sew on felt bottom.

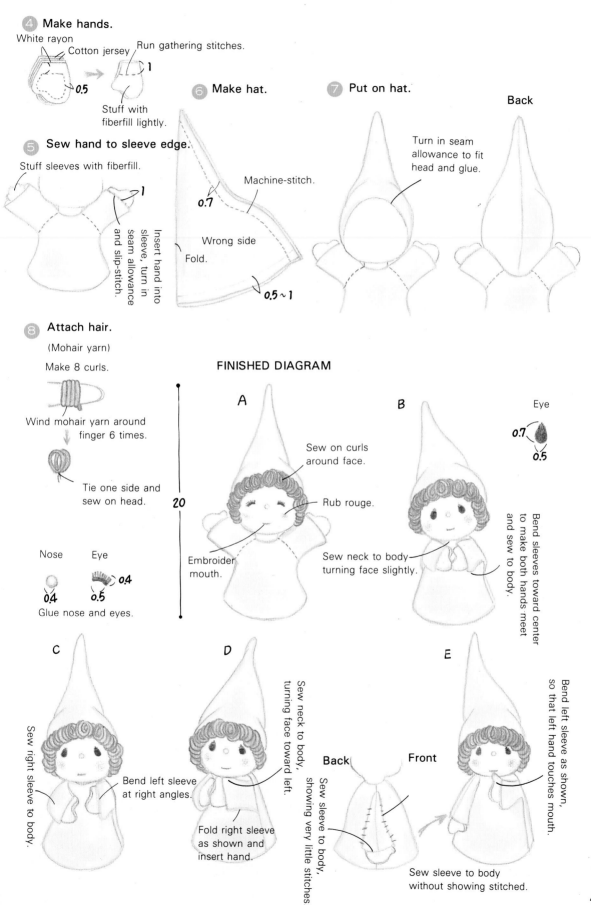

④ **Make hands.**

White rayon
Cotton jersey
Run gathering stitches.

0.5

Stuff with
fiberfill lightly.

⑤ **Sew hand to sleeve edge.**

Stuff sleeves with fiberfill.

1

Insert hand into
sleeve, turn in
seam allowance
and slip-stitch.

⑥ **Make hat.**

Machine-stitch.

0.7

Wrong side
Fold.

0.5～1

⑦ **Put on hat.**

Turn in seam
allowance to fit
head and glue.

Back

⑧ **Attach hair.**

(Mohair yarn)

Make 8 curls.

Wind mohair yarn around
finger 6 times.

Tie one side and
sew on head.

Nose   Eye
0.4

0.4   0.5

Glue nose and eyes.

FINISHED DIAGRAM

20

A

Sew on curls
around face.

Rub rouge.

Embroider
mouth.

B

Eye
0.7
0.5

Sew neck to body
turning face slightly.

Bend sleeves toward center
to make both hands meet
and sew to body.

C

Sew right sleeve
to body.

D

Bend left sleeve
at right angles.

Fold right sleeve
as shown and
insert hand.

Sew neck to body,
turning face toward left.

Back   Front

Sew sleeve to body,
showing very little stitches.

Sew sleeve to body
without showing stitched.

E

Bend left sleeve as shown,
so that left hand touches mouth.

45

Instructions on page 48.

Lovable Ornaments, shown on pages 46 & 47.

MATERIALS:

For face: See page 69.

[For each doll] For hands: White rayon and cotton jersey, 10 cm square each. For hair: Looped yarn. For stuffing: Polyester fiberfill.

[For Doll with Blue Hat] Felt (blue, 30 cm by 15 cm; white, 14 cm square); 2 ready-made appliqués; artificial flowers.

[For Doll with Bells] Felt (olive green and white, 14 cm square each; cream, 20 cm square); 2 ready-made appliqués; ribbon, 0.6 cm by 40 cm; plastic ring, 6.5 cm in diameter; 2 bells; artificial flowers.

[For Doll with Straw Hat] Felt (light orange and white,

14 cm square each); ribbon, 0.6 cm by 40 cm; straw hat, 16 cm in diameter; one bell; artificial flowers.

[For Dolls with Ring] Felt (white, 25 cm square; pink and purple, 14 cm square each); plastic ring, 14 cm in diameter; 2 ready-made appliqués; 2 buttons, 0.8 cm in diameter; 2 artificial flowers.

FINISHED SIZE: See diagrams.

DIRECTIONS:

Make face following instructions on pages 69–73. Attach head to body. Stuff body with fiberfill, turn in seam allowance and slip-stitch opening closed. Insert hands into sleeve edges and slip-stitch. Follow individual instructions for each doll.

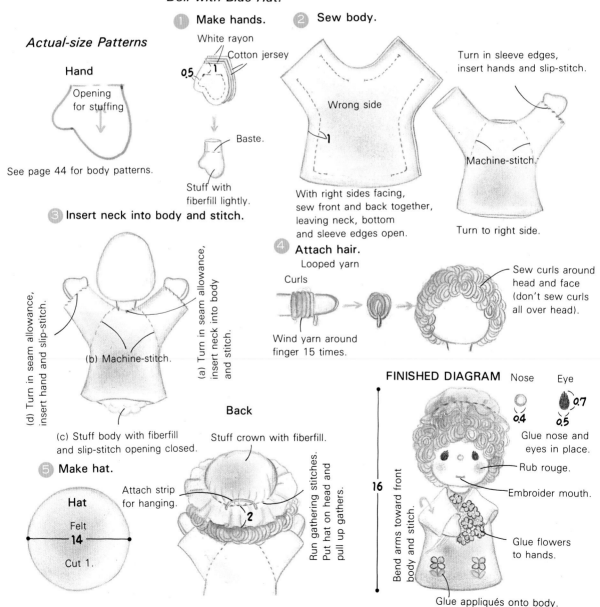

Doll with Blue Hat:

Actual-size Patterns

Hand

Opening for stuffing

See page 44 for body patterns.

1 **Make hands.**

White rayon
Cotton jersey

0.5

Baste.

Stuff with fiberfill lightly.

2 **Sew body.**

Wrong side

With right sides facing, sew front and back together, leaving neck, bottom and sleeve edges open.

Turn in sleeve edges, insert hands and slip-stitch.

Machine-stitch.

Turn to right side.

3 **Insert neck into body and stitch.**

(d) Turn in seam allowance, insert hand and slip-stitch.

(b) Machine-stitch.

(c) Stuff body with fiberfill and slip-stitch opening closed.

(a) Turn in seam allowance, insert neck into body and stitch.

4 **Attach hair.**

Looped yarn

Curls

Wind yarn around finger 15 times.

Sew curls around head and face (don't sew curls all over head).

5 **Make hat.**

Hat

Felt

14

Cut 1.

Attach strip for hanging.

Back

Stuff crown with fiberfill.

Run gathering stitches. Put hat on head and pull up gathers.

FINISHED DIAGRAM

Nose
0.4

Eye
0.7
0.5

Glue nose and eyes in place.

Rub rouge.

Embroider mouth.

Glue flowers to hands.

Glue appliqués onto body.

16

Bend arms toward front body and stitch.

Doll over Straw Hat:

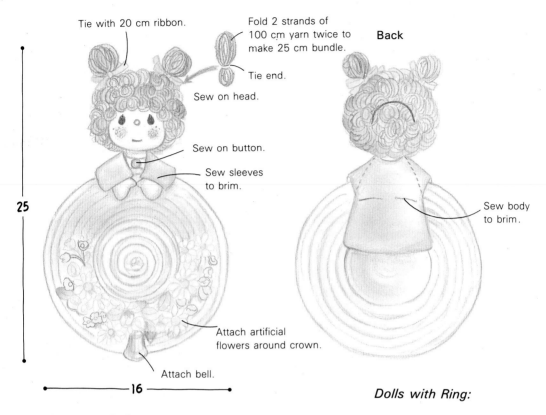

Tie with 20 cm ribbon.

Fold 2 strands of 100 cm yarn twice to make 25 cm bundle.

Tie end.

Sew on head.

Back

Sew on button.

Sew sleeves to brim.

Sew body to brim.

25

Attach artificial flowers around crown.

Attach bell.

16

Dolls with Ring:

Doll with Bells:

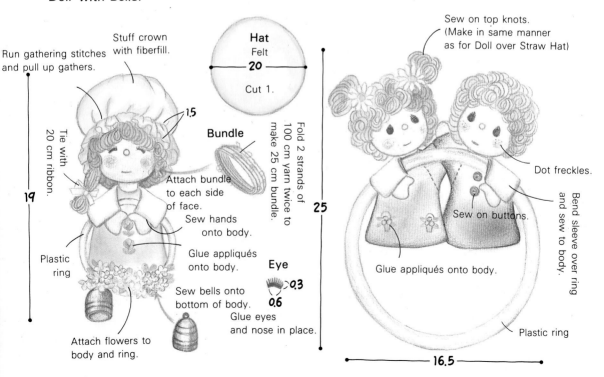

Run gathering stitches and pull up gathers.

Stuff crown with fiberfill.

Hat
Felt
20
Cut 1.

Sew on top knots.
(Make in same manner as for Doll over Straw Hat)

1.5

Tie with 20 cm ribbon.

Bundle

Fold 2 strands of 100 cm yarn twice to make 25 cm bundle.

Attach bundle to each side of face.

Sew hands onto body.

Glue appliqués onto body.

Eye

Dot freckles.

Sew on buttons.

Bend sleeve over ring and sew to body.

19

Plastic ring

0.3

0.6

Sew bells onto bottom of body.

Glue eyes and nose in place.

25

Glue appliqués onto body.

Attach flowers to body and ring.

Plastic ring

16.5

M
y Family

Instructions on page 52.

My Family, shown on pages 50 & 51.

MATERIALS:	Mother	Grandmother	Grandfather	Father	Brother	Sister	Me	DIRECTIONS:
For each doll	For face: See page 69. One stick Polyester fiberfill Felt-tipped pen in black 3-ply yarn							Make face following instructions on pages 69–73. Cut body pieces adding 1 cm for seam allowance. Follow individual instructions for each doll.
Cotton fabric	25×12	25×12	20×15	26×16	26×16	20×10	20×10	
Wire #20 for glasses			20cm	20cm				
FINISHED SIZE	14.5cm	13.5cm	16.5cm	19cm	19cm	12cm	12cm	

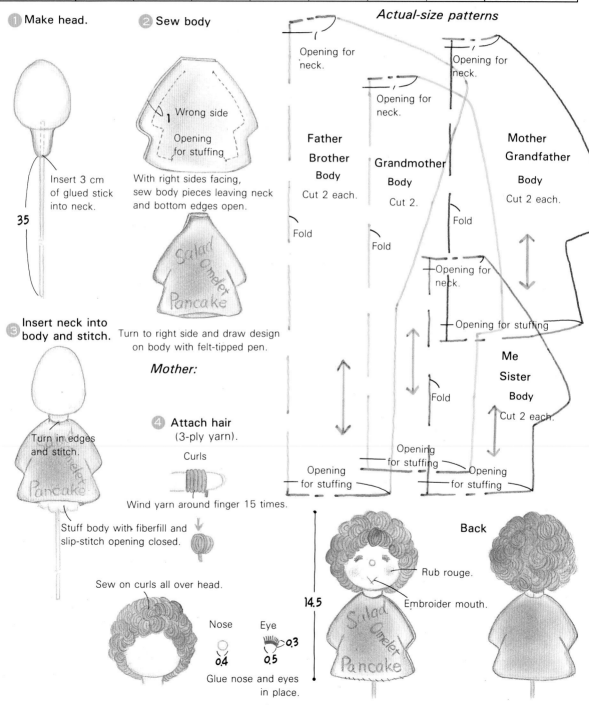

Actual-size patterns

1 Make head.

Insert 3 cm of glued stick into neck.

35

2 Sew body

Wrong side

Opening for stuffing

With right sides facing, sew body pieces leaving neck and bottom edges open.

Turn to right side and draw design on body with felt-tipped pen.

Mother:

3 Insert neck into body and stitch.

Turn in edges and stitch.

Stuff body with fiberfill and slip-stitch opening closed.

4 Attach hair (3-ply yarn).

Curls

Wind yarn around finger 15 times.

Sew on curls all over head.

Nose
0.4

Eye
0.3
0.5

Glue nose and eyes in place.

Opening for neck.

Opening for neck.

Opening for neck.

Opening for neck.

**Father
Brother
Body**
Cut 2 each.

Fold

**Grandmother
Body**
Cut 2.

Fold

**Mother
Grandfather
Body**
Cut 2 each.

Fold

Opening for stuffing

**Me
Sister
Body**
Cut 2 each.

Fold

Opening for stuffing

Opening for stuffing

Opening for stuffing

14.5

Rub rouge.

Embroider mouth.

Back

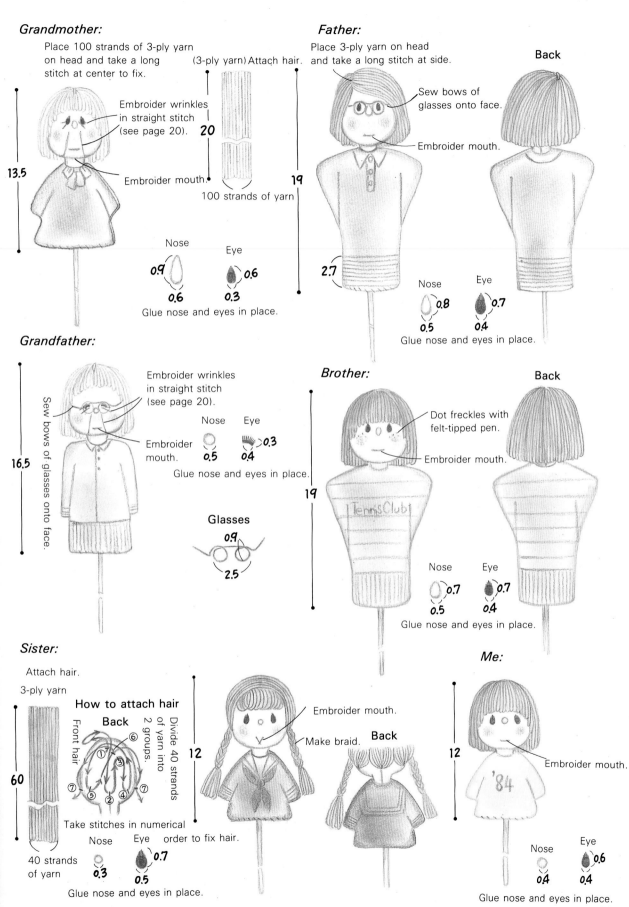

Grandmother:

Place 100 strands of 3-ply yarn on head and take a long stitch at center to fix.

Embroider wrinkles in straight stitch (see page 20).

Embroider mouth.

13.5

(3-ply yarn) Attach hair.

20

100 strands of yarn

19

Nose
0.9
0.6

Eye
0.6
0.3

Glue nose and eyes in place.

Father:

Place 3-ply yarn on head and take a long stitch at side.

Sew bows of glasses onto face.

Embroider mouth.

Back

2.7

Nose
0.8
0.5

Eye
0.7
0.4

Glue nose and eyes in place.

Grandfather:

Embroider wrinkles in straight stitch (see page 20).

Embroider mouth.

Sew bows of glasses onto face.

16.5

Nose
0.5

Eye
0.3
0.4

Glue nose and eyes in place.

Glasses
0.9
2.5

Brother:

Dot freckles with felt-tipped pen.

Embroider mouth.

Back

TennisClub

19

Nose
0.7
0.5

Eye
0.7
0.4

Glue nose and eyes in place.

Sister:

Attach hair.
3-ply yarn

How to attach hair

Back

Front hair

Divide 40 strands of yarn into 2 groups.

60

Take stitches in numerical order to fix hair.

40 strands of yarn

Nose
0.3

Eye
0.7
0.5

Glue nose and eyes in place.

Embroider mouth.

Make braid.

Back

12

Me:

12

Embroider mouth.

'84

Nose
0.4

Eye
0.6
0.4

Glue nose and eyes in place.

Chorus Group

Instructions on page 56.

Chorus Group, shown on pages 54 & 55.

MATERIALS:	A	B	C	D	E	F	G	H	DIRECTIONS:
For each doll	For face: See page 69. Heavyweight iron-on interfacing.				Polyester fiberfill. 3-ply yarn. Self-covered button, 0.9 cm in diameter.				Make face following instructions on pages 69–73. Follow individual instructions for each doll.
Corduroy	58 × 8 18 × 7	58 × 8 18 × 7	60 × 10 18 × 7	60 × 10 18 × 7	60 × 10 18 × 7	62 × 10 18 × 7	64 × 8 18 × 7	64 × 8 18 × 7	
Cotton checks.	40 × 10	40 × 10	40 × 10	40 × 10	50 × 10	42 × 10	40 × 10	48 × 10	
Button, 0.4 cm in diameter.	2	2	2	3	3	2	2	2	

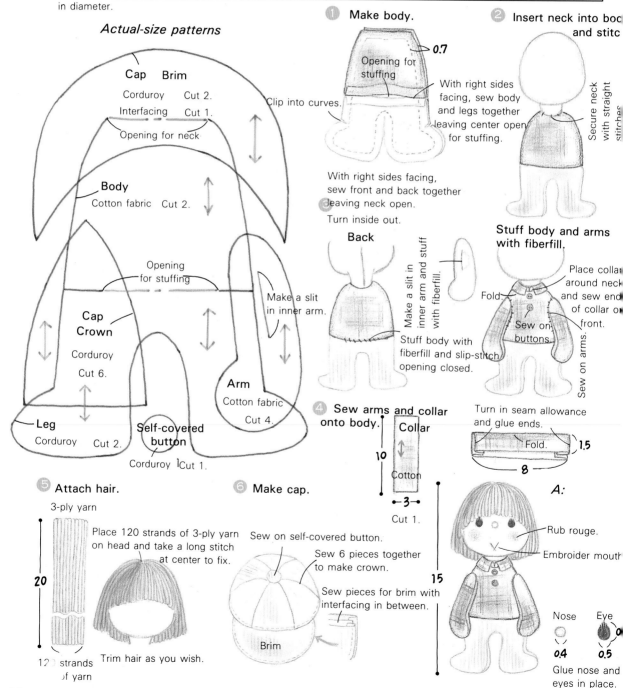

Actual-size patterns

Cap Brim
Corduroy Cut 2.
Interfacing Cut 1.
Opening for neck

Body
Cotton fabric Cut 2.

Opening for stuffing

Cap Crown
Corduroy Cut 6.

Leg
Corduroy Cut 2.

Self-covered button
Corduroy Cut 1.

Make a slit in inner arm.

Arm
Cotton fabric Cut 4.

① Make body.

0.7

Opening for stuffing

With right sides facing, sew body and legs together leaving center open for stuffing.

Clip into curves.

With right sides facing, sew front and back together leaving neck open.

Turn inside out.

Back

Make a slit in inner arm and stuff with fiberfill.

Stuff body with fiberfill and slip-stitch opening closed.

② Insert neck into body and stitch.

Secure neck with straight stitches.

③ Stuff body and arms with fiberfill.

Place collar around neck and sew end of collar on front.

Fold

Sew on buttons.

Sew on arms.

Turn in seam allowance and glue ends.

Fold. 1.5

8

④ Sew arms and collar onto body.

Collar
10
Cotton
3
Cut 1.

⑤ Attach hair.

3-ply yarn

Place 120 strands of 3-ply yarn on head and take a long stitch at center to fix.

20

120 strands of yarn

Trim hair as you wish.

⑥ Make cap.

Sew on self-covered button.

Sew 6 pieces together to make crown.

Sew pieces for brim with interfacing in between.

Brim

A:

Rub rouge.

Embroider mouth

15

Nose
0.4

Eye
0.5

Glue nose and eyes in place.

56

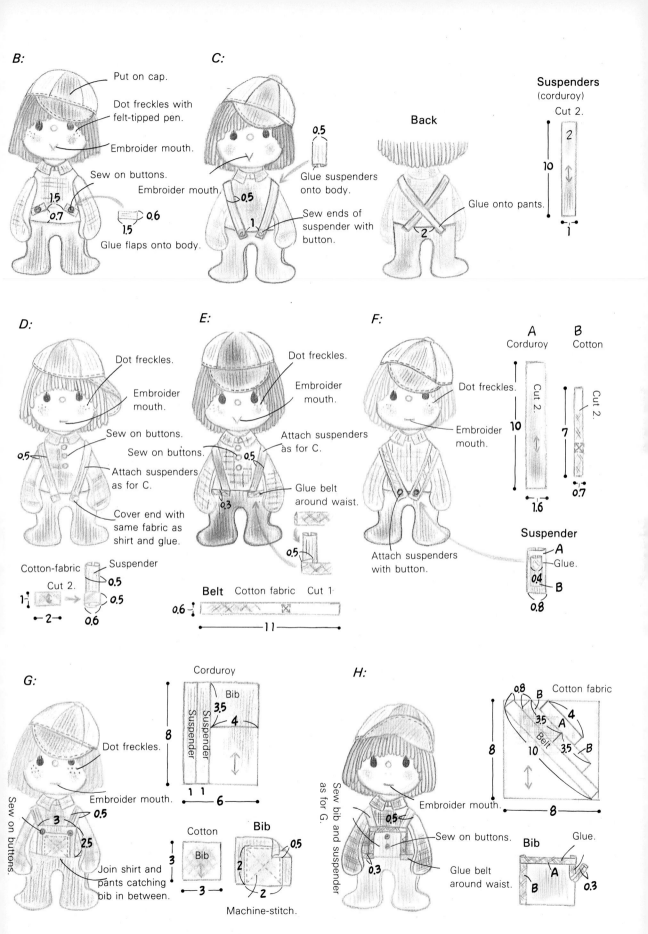

B:

Put on cap.

Dot freckles with felt-tipped pen.

Embroider mouth.

Sew on buttons.

1.5

0.7

1.5

0.6

Glue flaps onto body.

C:

0.5

Embroider mouth.

0.5

Glue suspenders onto body.

1

Sew ends of suspender with button.

Back

Glue onto pants.

2

Suspenders
(corduroy)
Cut 2.

2

10

1

D:

Dot freckles.

Embroider mouth.

Sew on buttons.

0.5

Attach suspenders as for C.

Cover end with same fabric as shirt and glue.

Cotton-fabric

Cut 2.

Suspender

0.5

0.5

1

2

0.6

E:

Dot freckles.

Embroider mouth.

Sew on buttons.

0.5

0.3

Attach suspenders as for C.

Glue belt around waist.

0.5

Belt Cotton fabric Cut 1·

0.6

11

F:

Dot freckles.

Embroider mouth.

Attach suspenders with button.

A
Corduroy

Cut 2.

10

1.6

B
Cotton

Cut 2.

7

0.7

Suspender

A

Glue.

0.4

B

0.8

G:

Dot freckles.

Embroider mouth.

Sew on buttons.

3

0.5

2.5

Join shirt and pants catching bib in between.

Corduroy

Bib

3.5

4

Suspender

Suspender

8

1 1

6

Cotton

Bib

3

3

Bib

0.5

2

2

Machine-stitch.

H:

Sew bib and suspender as for G.

Embroider mouth.

0.5

0.3

Sew on buttons.

Glue belt around waist.

0.8

B

4

3.5

A

Belt

B

3.5

10

Cotton fabric

8

8

Bib

A

Glue.

B

0.3

57

*P*ink Dolls

Instructions on page 60.

Pink Dolls, shown on pages 58 & 59.

MATERIALS:

For face: See page 69.

[For each doll] For body: Satin quilted fabric, 50 cm by 16 cm; felt, 11 cm by 10 cm; thick cardboard, 11 cm by 10 cm. For hair: Bouclé yarn. For stuffing: Polyester fiberfill.

[For Doll with Bouquet] Lace edging, 3 cm by 95 cm; ribbon, 1.8 cm by 30 cm; 24 artificial flowers.

[For Doll with Parasol] Lace edging, 3 cm by 15 cm; ribbon, 0.6 cm by 260 cm; 3 ready-made appliqués; lace edging for bag, 3 cm by 15 cm; wire #18, 11 cm; silver lamé thread.

[For Doll with Bag] Floral braid, 48 cm; lace edging for bag, 3 cm by 10 cm; 6 artificial flowers; silver lamé thread.

FINISHED SIZE: 19 cm tall.

DIRECTIONS:

Make face following instructions on pages 69–73. Insert neck into body and stitch. Stuff body with fiberfill. Place cardboard at bottom, pull up gathers and slip-stitch felt onto bottom. Follow individual instructions for each doll.

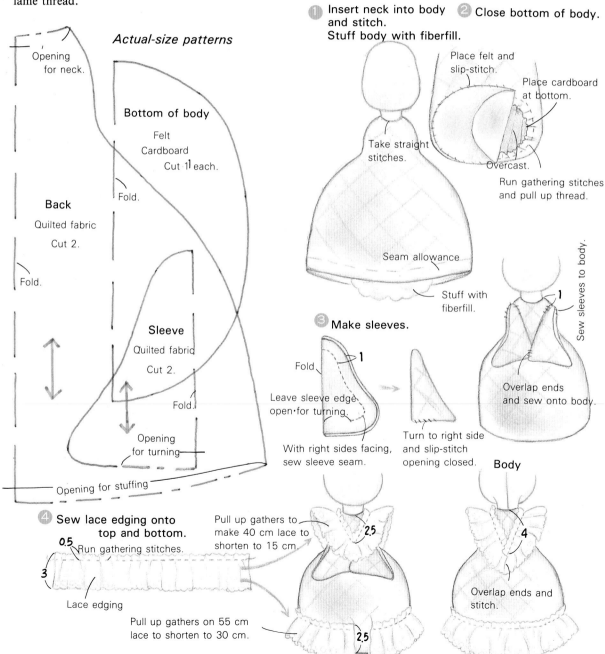

Actual-size patterns

Opening for neck.

Bottom of body
Felt
Cardboard
Cut 1 each.

Fold.

Back
Quilted fabric
Cut 2.

Fold.

Sleeve
Quilted fabric
Cut 2.

Fold.

Opening for turning.

Opening for stuffing

① Insert neck into body and stitch.
Stuff body with fiberfill.

② Close bottom of body.

Place felt and slip-stitch.

Place cardboard at bottom.

Take straight stitches.

Overcast.

Run gathering stitches and pull up thread.

Seam allowance

Stuff with fiberfill.

③ Make sleeves.

Fold

Leave sleeve edge open for turning.

With right sides facing, sew sleeve seam.

Turn to right side and slip-stitch opening closed.

Sew sleeves to body.

Overlap ends and sew onto body.

Body

④ Sew lace edging onto top and bottom.

0.5 Run gathering stitches.

3

Lace edging

Pull up gathers on 55 cm lace to shorten to 30 cm.

Pull up gathers to make 40 cm lace to shorten to 15 cm.

2.5

Overlap ends and stitch.

2.5

⑤ Attach hair and make features.

Doll with Bouquet:
FINISHED DIAGRAM

Hair (bouclé yarn)

How to attach hair
Back

Front hair

① Start.
②
⑧ ⑦ ④ ⑧
⑥ ③ ⑤

120

30 strands
of yarn

Take stitches in numerical order
to fix 30 strands of yarn.

Nose
0.4

Eye
0.7
0.4

Glue nose and eyes in place.

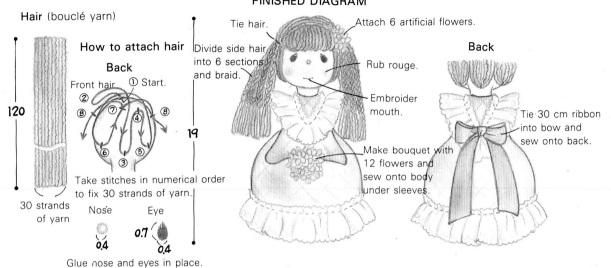

Tie hair.

Divide side hair
into 6 sections
and braid.

Attach 6 artificial flowers.

Rub rouge.

Embroider
mouth.

Make bouquet with
12 flowers and
sew onto body
under sleeves.

Back

Tie 30 cm ribbon
into bow and
sew onto back.

19

Doll with Parasol:

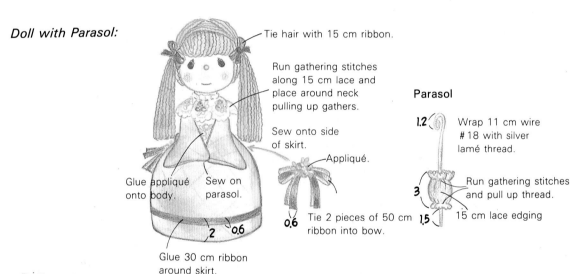

Tie hair with 15 cm ribbon.

Run gathering stitches
along 15 cm lace and
place around neck
pulling up gathers.

Sew onto side
of skirt.

Glue appliqué
onto body.

Sew on
parasol.

Appliqué.

Tie 2 pieces of 50 cm
ribbon into bow.

0.6
0.6

Glue 30 cm ribbon
around skirt.

2   0.6

Parasol

Wrap 11 cm wire
#18 with silver
lamé thread.

1.2

Run gathering stitches
and pull up thread.

3

15 cm lace edging

1.5

Doll with Bag:

Divide hair into
8 sections, fold each
to half and fasten
each end.

Sew on handle of bag
under sleeve.

Attach 3 artificial flowers
on top of curls.

Glue 46 cm
floral braid.

2

1   2.5

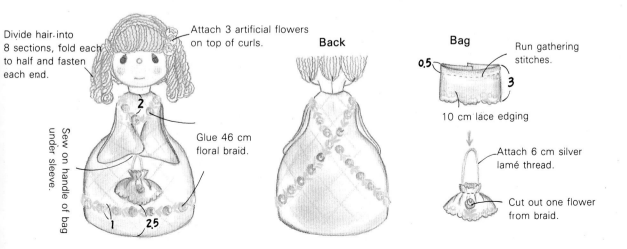

Back

Bag

Run gathering
stitches.

0.5

3

10 cm lace edging

Attach 6 cm silver
lamé thread.

Cut out one flower
from braid.

Characters from Storybooks

Instructions on page 64.

Characters from Storybooks,

shown on pages 62 & 63.

MATERIALS:

For face: See page 69.

[For each doll] Polyester fiberfill; cardboard tube (use cardboard core from wrapper or waxed paper).

[For Captain of Viking Ship] Cotton stripes, 16 cm by 8 cm; cotton print, 15 cm square; solid, 15 cm by 7 cm; scrap of black felt; looped yarn.

[For Fairy] Cotton print, 19 cm by 14 cm; silver braid, 0.4 cm by 20 cm; 2 bells; wire #20; 2 leaves; bulky yarn.

[For Prince] Cotton prints, 16 cm square and 22 cm by 14 cm; ribbon, 1.8 cm by 15 cm; braid, 0.8 cm by 28 cm; one button, 1 cm in diameter; one pair of earrings.

[For Russian Poet] Cotton print, 16 cm by 8 cm; denim, 15 cm by 8 cm; felt, 19 cm by 10 cm; Tyrolean tape, 0.6 cm by 15 cm; 3-ply yarn.

[For French Count] Satin, 16 cm by 8 cm: velveteen, 15 cm by 8 cm; braid, 2.2 cm by 25 cm; lace edging, 2.5 cm by 30 cm; ribbon, 1 cm by 25 cm; ready-made appliqué; looped yarn.

[For King of Tropical Island] Cotton jersey, 16 cm by 8 cm; cotton yarn; artificial flowers; looped yarn.

[For Witch] Cotton broadcloth: black, 25 cm by 36 cm and lavender, 10 cm by 36 cm; ribbon, 0.6 cm by 30 cm; one ready-made appliqué; 2 artificial flowers; looped yarn.

FINISHED SIZE: See diagrams.

DIRECTIONS:

Make face following instructions on pages 69–73. Insert head into body and stitch. Stuff body with fiberfill. Insert body into cloth-covered cardboard tube. Follow individual instructions for each doll.

Actual-size patterns

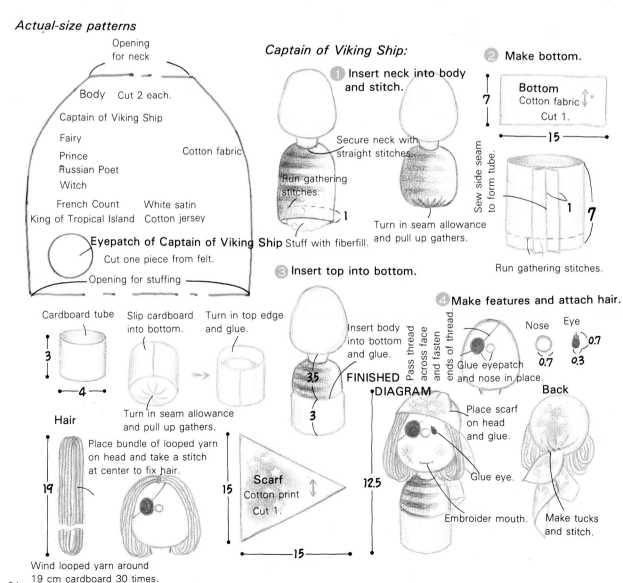

Opening for neck

Body Cut 2 each.

Captain of Viking Ship

Fairy

Prince

Russian Poet

Witch

French Count   White satin

King of Tropical Island Cotton jersey

Cotton fabric

Eyepatch of Captain of Viking Ship

Cut one piece from felt.

Opening for stuffing

Cardboard tube

Slip cardboard into bottom.

Turn in top edge and glue.

3

4

Turn in seam allowance and pull up gathers.

Hair

19

Wind looped yarn around 19 cm cardboard 30 times.

Place bundle of looped yarn on head and take a stitch at center to fix hair.

Captain of Viking Ship:

1 Insert neck into body and stitch.

Secure neck with straight stitches.

Run gathering stitches.

1

Stuff with fiberfill.

Turn in seam allowance and pull up gathers.

2 Make bottom.

7

Bottom
Cotton fabric
Cut 1.

15

Sew side seam to form tube.

1   7

Run gathering stitches.

3 Insert top into bottom.

Insert body into bottom and glue.

3.5

3

FINISHED DIAGRAM

Pass thread across face and fasten ends of thread.

15

Scarf
Cotton print
Cut 1.

15

12.5

4 Make features and attach hair.

Nose   Eye

0.7   0.7 0.3

Glue eyepatch and nose in place.

Back

Place scarf on head and glue.

Glue eye.

Embroider mouth.

Make tucks and stitch.

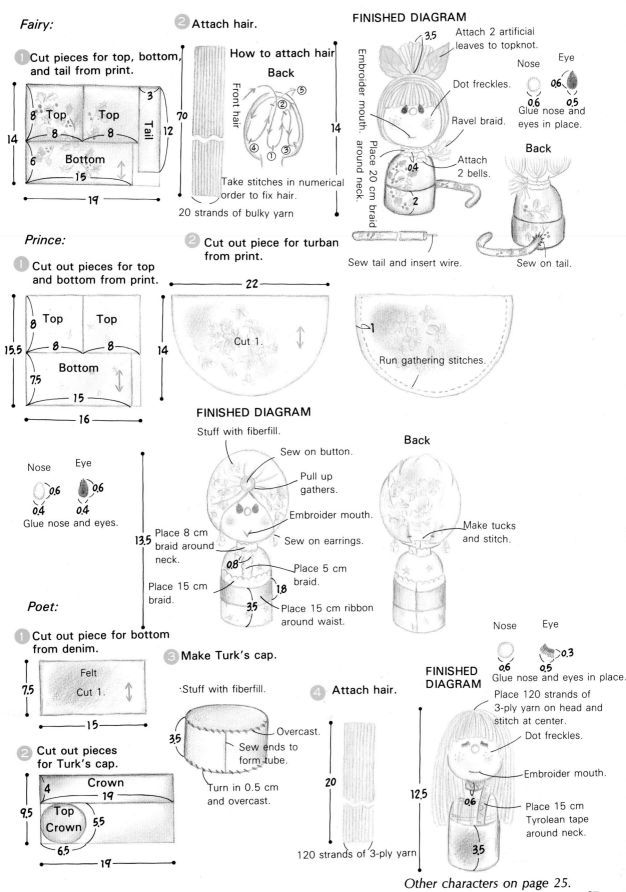

Fairy:

1 Cut pieces for top, bottom, and tail from print.

14 — 19
8 Top | Top | 3
8 | 8 | Tail | 12
6
Bottom
15

2 Attach hair.

70

How to attach hair

Front hair

Back

⑤ ② ④ ① ③

Take stitches in numerical order to fix hair.

20 strands of bulky yarn

14

FINISHED DIAGRAM

3.5
Attach 2 artificial leaves to topknot.

Embroider mouth.

Place 20 cm braid around neck.

Dot freckles.

Ravel braid.

0.4

Attach 2 bells.

2

Sew tail and insert wire.

Nose   **Eye**

0.6   0.6   0.5

Glue nose and eyes in place.

Back

Sew on tail.

Prince:

1 Cut out pieces for top and bottom from print.

15.5
8 Top | Top
8 | 8
7.5
Bottom
15
14
16

2 Cut out piece for turban from print.

22
Cut 1.

1
Run gathering stitches.

Nose   **Eye**
0.6   0.6
0.4   0.4
Glue nose and eyes.

FINISHED DIAGRAM

Stuff with fiberfill.

Sew on button.

Pull up gathers.

Embroider mouth.

Sew on earrings.

13.5

Place 8 cm braid around neck.

Place 15 cm braid.

0.8

Place 5 cm braid.

1.8

3.5

Place 15 cm ribbon around waist.

Back

Make tucks and stitch.

Poet:

1 Cut out piece for bottom from denim.

7.5
Felt
Cut 1.
15

2 Cut out pieces for Turk's cap.

4 Crown
19
9.5 Top Crown 5.5
6.5
19

3 Make Turk's cap.

:Stuff with fiberfill.

3.5

Overcast.
Sew ends to form tube.

Turn in 0.5 cm and overcast.

4 Attach hair.

20

120 strands of 3-ply yarn

Nose   **Eye**
0.3
0.6   0.5
Glue nose and eyes in place.

FINISHED DIAGRAM

Place 120 strands of 3-ply yarn on head and stitch at center.

Dot freckles.

Embroider mouth.

12.5

0.6

Place 15 cm Tyrolean tape around neck.

3.5

Other characters on page 25.

Instructions on page 68.

Step-by-step Instructions for Doll Making.
Let's make Seamstresses shown on pages 66 & 67.

The same face pattern is used for all the 100 dolls in this book. However, you can make many different dolls by changing the amount of stuffing, facial expressions, hairstyles, clothes, and so on.

In these pages, we will show you basic techniques of doll making. Once you have mastered the basics, you can easily make the dolls you want.

1. Prepare the following materials for one seamstress.

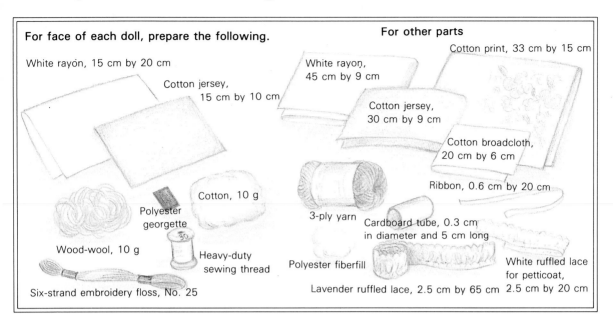

For face of each doll, prepare the following.

White rayon, 15 cm by 20 cm

Cotton jersey, 15 cm by 10 cm

Polyester georgette

Cotton, 10 g

Wood-wool, 10 g

Heavy-duty sewing thread

Six-strand embroidery floss, No. 25

For other parts

Cotton print, 33 cm by 15 cm

White rayon, 45 cm by 9 cm

Cotton jersey, 30 cm by 9 cm

Cotton broadcloth, 20 cm by 6 cm

Ribbon, 0.6 cm by 20 cm

3-ply yarn

Cardboard tube, 0.3 cm in diameter and 5 cm long

Polyester fiberfill

Lavender ruffled lace, 2.5 cm by 65 cm

White ruffled lace for petticoat, 2.5 cm by 20 cm

Cotton, wood-wool, and white rayon are used for making the foundation of the face, which is the most important part of each doll. For stuffing the body, cotton, wood-wool, and polyester fiberfill are used but the amount may differ with each doll maker; just be sure to prepare a sufficient amount of stuffing. All the dolls in this book are made using the same face pattern and the materials shown above, while the body patterns change for each doll. For clothing try to use leftover fabrics, lace edgings, or whatever you may have on hand.

Actual-size pattern

Opening for stuffing

Back of head

White rayon

Cut 2 pieces.

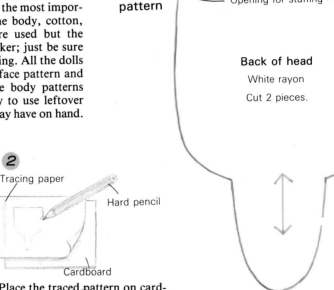

1

Place a sheet of tracing paper on the book and trace the pattern.

2

Tracing paper

Hard pencil

Cardboard

Place the traced pattern on cardboard and trace with a hard pencil or a dry ballpoint pen.

3

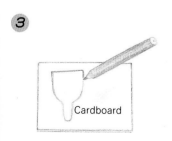

Cardboard

Draw along traced lines with a pencil.

4

Cut out the pattern with sharp scissors.

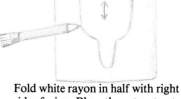

White rayon

Fold white rayon in half with right sides facing. Place the cut-out pattern on white rayon and trace.

2. Make back of head.

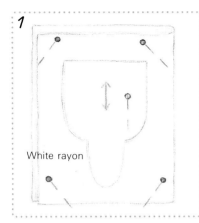

1

White rayon

Machine-stitch all around leaving top open for stuffing. Backstitch beginning and ending.

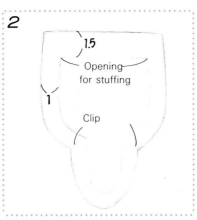

2

1.5
Opening for stuffing
1
Clip

Add 1.5 cm to top edge and 1 cm to other edge for seam allowance. Clip into corners and turn to right side using a small screwdriver.

3

Stuff firmly with wood-wool pushing with a big screwdriver. Carefully push remaining wood-wool with hands up to finished line.

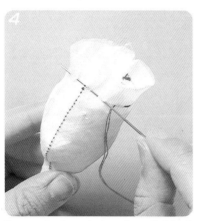

4

Run gathering stitches along finished line with double strands of heavy-duty sewing thread. Overlap last and first stitches.

5

Turn in seam allowance, pull up gathers and fasten thread but don't cut off.

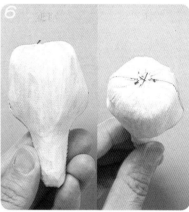

6

Continue to close top, crossing, stitches. Fasten thread again.

3. Make foundation of face.

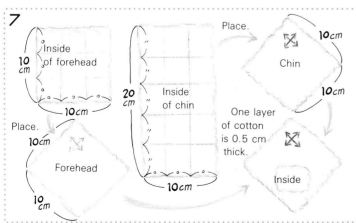

7

Inside of forehead
10 cm
10 cm
Place.
10 cm
Forehead
10 cm

20 cm
Inside of chin
10 cm

Place.
10 cm
Chin
10 cm

One layer of cotton is 0.5 cm thick.
10 cm
Inside

Tear cotton the required size and 0.5 cm thick. Lay 2 pieces of cotton together as shown. Use your hands to tear cotton.

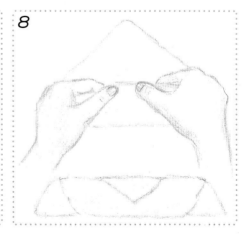

8

Roll up cotton tightly, smoothing overlapped area.

9

Place rolled cotton for chin on back of head between side seams.

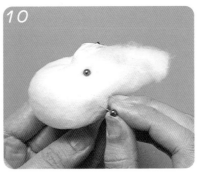

10

Pin cotton to back of head, shaping cotton as shown.

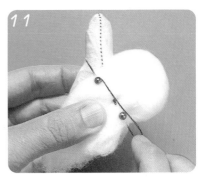

11

Using 6 cm-long needle and double strands of heavy-duty sewing thread, sew cotton onto back of head.

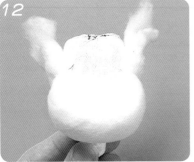

12

Front of chin

13

Place rolled cotton for forehead over chin.

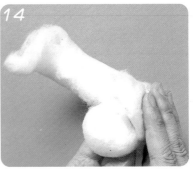

14

Fold extra cotton for chin upward. upward.

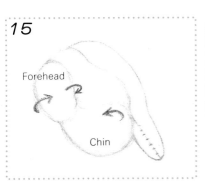

15

Forehead

Chin

Turn in extra cotton for forehead.

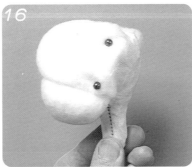

16

Pin forehead to each side of head.

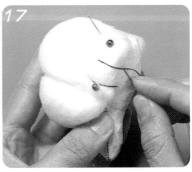

17

Using 6 cm-long needle and double strands of heavy-duty thread, take 3 stitches, catching back of head.

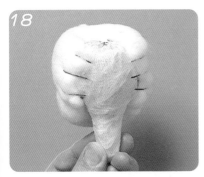

18

Half-finished foundation of face (back)

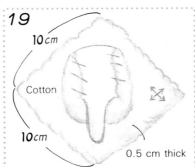

19

10 cm

Cotton

10 cm

0.5 cm thick

Tear off 10 cm square cotton on the bias and place half-finished foundation at center of the square as shown.

20

Cover face with cotton, starting from chin.
Pull cotton carefully so as not to make wrinkles around chin.

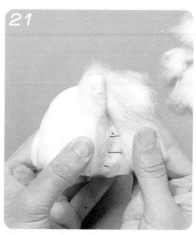

Cover neck and overlap cotton at back of neck.

Tear off extra cotton at top.

Finished foundation of face: It is important to make smooth line from chin to neck.

4. Cover foundation of face with cotton jersey.

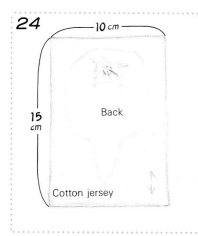

24

— 10 cm —

15 cm

Back

Cotton jersey

Cover foundation of face with cotton jersey matching grain.

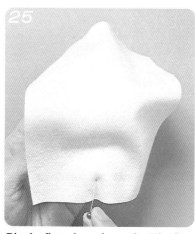

Pin the first pin under neck. (The first pin is very important.)

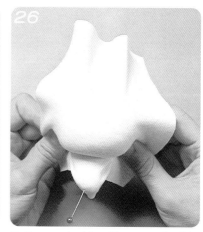

Pull up each side of jersey to fit chin as tight as possible.

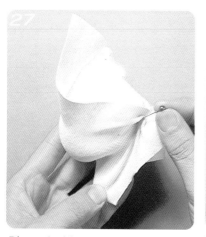

Pin each side securely.

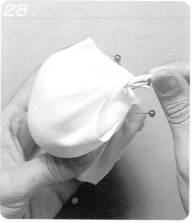

Twist top part of jersey toward back and pin.

Back of head

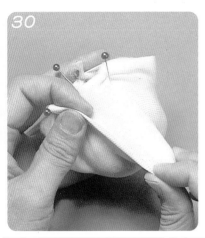

Tuck in extra fabric at center back and pin.

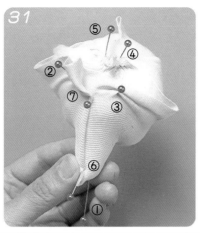

You must pin in numerical order from 1 to 7 as shown.

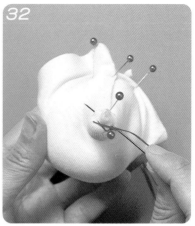

Using 6 cm-long needle and one strand of heavy-duty sewing thread, close opening at bottom of neck, catching foundation.

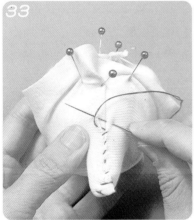

Continue to stitch upward to No. 7 pin, but stitch cotton jersey only. Take last stitch catching foundation and make knot.

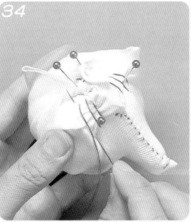

Using double strands of heavy-duty sewing thread, take long stitches at left and right sides catching foundation

Sew twisted parts of top (see steps 4 & 5) to foundation.

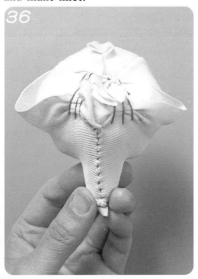

Finished head (back)

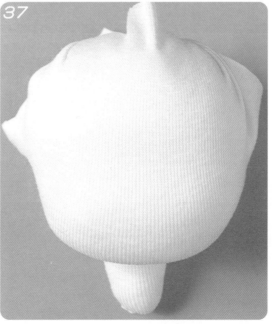

The picture at left is an actual-size face. Use it for comparison to your doll, although the size of a finished face can differ even when the same materials are used. Try to make slim face for boy, fat cheeks for baby and small face for grown-up by increasing or decreasing stuffing.

5. Assemble body.

Actual-size pattern

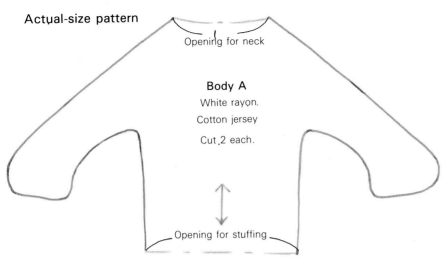

Opening for neck

Body A

White rayon.

Cotton jersey

Cut 2 each.

Opening for stuffing

1 With right sides of cotton-jersey facing and white rayon on both sides, machine-stitch all around leaving neck and bottom open. Backstitch beginning and ending.

2 Cut out sewn body adding 0.5 cm all around. Clip into curves. Turn inside out.

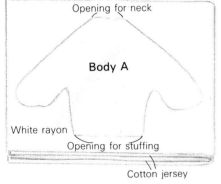

Opening for neck

Body A

White rayon

Opening for stuffing

Cotton jersey

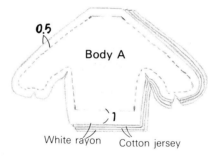

0.5

Body A

1

White rayon   Cotton jersey

3 Sew neck to body and stuff with fiberfill.

4 Close opening.

5 Insert body into cardboard tube.

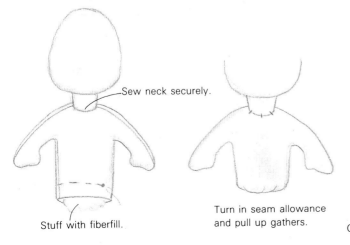

Sew neck securely.

Stuff with fiberfill.

Turn in seam allowance and pull up gathers.

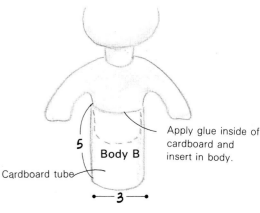

5

Cardboard tube

Body B

Apply glue inside of cardboard and insert in body.

3

6 Cover cardboard with white rayon.

Body B   White rayon

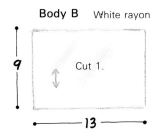

9

Cut 1.

13

Cover cardboard with white rayon.

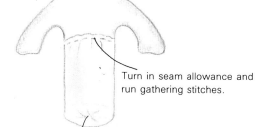

Sew white rayon into tube.

Run gathering stitches.

1

1

Turn in seam allowance and run gathering stitches.

Pull up gathers.

8 Put petticoat on body.

7 Cut out one piece for petticoat.

White broadcloth

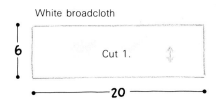

6

Cut 1.

20

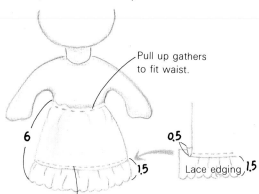

Pull up gathers to fit waist.

6

0.5

1.5

Lace edging 1.5

Sew on 20 cm ruffled lace.

6. Put on dress.

9 Cut out pieces of dress and hat.

Print

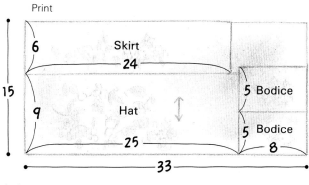

6

Skirt

24

15

9

Hat

25

5 Bodice

5 Bodice

8

33

10 Sew dress.

0.5

3.5

0.5

14 cm ruffled lace

End of stitching

0.5

1.5

5.5

Gather skirt and sew to bodice.

1.5

Sew on 24 cm ruffled lace.

11 Put dress on body.

Front

Sew back bodice onto body.

Make a slit at top of cnter front.

Back

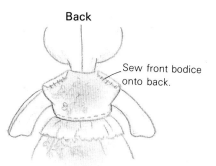

Sew front bodice onto back.

12 Make hat.

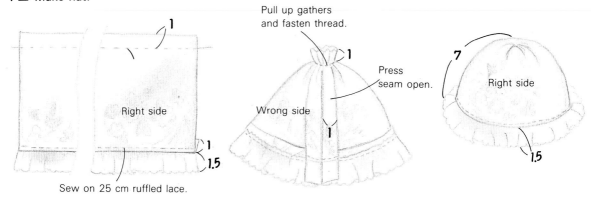

Sew on 25 cm ruffled lace.

Pull up gathers and fasten thread.

Press seam open.

Right side

Wrong side

Right side

7. Attach hair.

Choose soft color of yarn for hair. When making curls, be careful not to make them too big or too small. Don't crowd the curls in order not to lose the softness of curly hair.

1

Hair (3-ply yarn)

150 strands of yarn

30

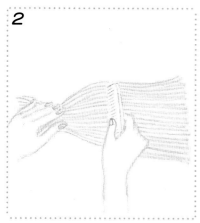

Place 150 strands of yarn on working table and comb with a large-tooth comb.

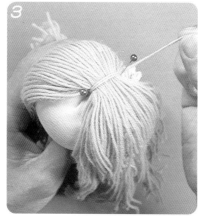

Place combed yarn on head matching centers and pin. With double strands of same yarn, take a stitch at center securely.

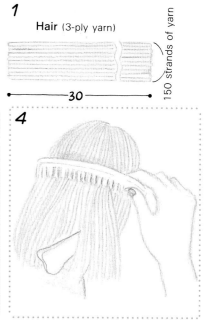

Spread yarn all over head, combing.

Apply glue to front and back of head. Comb yarn again.

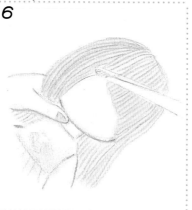

Trim yarn to fit doll's face.

Finished hair

8. Make features.

Actual-size nose and eyes

0.6

0.3   0.4

Making features is one of the important parts of doll making. Before fixing eyes or nose with glue, place them on face in different places. In moving these parts around you will find your favorite face. Then, mark with pencil and fix them with glue.

1

Draw out horizontal threads.

With sharp scissors, cut out tear-drop shapes on the grain for eyes.

2

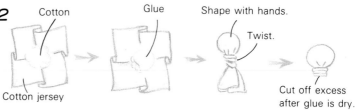

Cotton

Glue

Shape with hands.

Twist.

Cotton jersey

Cut off excess after glue is dry.

Use cotton for stuffing and match the grain of nose with that of face.

The features of the doll you are making reflect your feelings. When you are sad, your doll will look sad. When you are high-spirited, your doll's face will be lively and cheerful. Therefore, try to make the features when you feel happy.

3

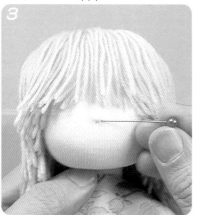

Pick up nose with pin and apply glue with fingertip. Place nose on face.

4

Glue eyes onto face using pin.

5

Using 6 cm-long needle and double strands of pink embroidery floss, insert needle from left side of face. Tie knot at the end of thread.

6

Embroider mouth and bring out needle from right side. Pull thread tightly and fasten thread.

7

Apply rouge on cotton and rub cheeks.

8

15

Finished doll

9. Make 4 more dolls in same manner.

Use the following lace edgings, tapes, or ribbons for each doll.
Other materials are the same as the above doll.

For doll with Green Dress: Ruffled lace, 2.5 cm by 24 cm and 3 cm by 25 cm.

For Doll with Peony Rose Dress: Ruffled lace, 2.5 cm by 24 cm; Tyrolean tape, 1.5 cm by 5 cm; ribbon, 0.6 cm by 30 cm.

For Doll with Yellow Dress: Ruffled lace, 2.5 cm by 24 cm and 3 cm by 44 cm; ribbon, 0.6 cm by 15 cm.

For Doll with Blue Dress: Ruffled lace, 2.5 cm by 50 cm; ribbon, 0.6 cm by 20 cm.

DIRECTIONS: Make as for the first doll. Choose a color of yarn for hair that matches dress.

Doll with Green Dress

Doll with Peony Rose Dress

Hat

2.5

Turn up.

Ruffled lace, 3 cm wide

1.8

Ruffled lace

Tie 10 strands of yarn with 15 cm ribbon.

Sew Tyrolean tape onto center front.

1

1.5

Ruffled lace

Doll with Yellow Dress

Hat

Ruffled lace 2.3

1.5

Ruffled lace

0.6

2.3

Ruffled lace

Tie 15 cm ribbon into bow and sew on.

Doll with Blue Dress

Tie 20 cm ribbon into bow and glue.

Hair

20

150 strands of 3-ply yarn

Hat

1.5

Ruffled lace

1.5

Ruffled lace

General Information about Doll Making

● MATERIALS AND TOOLS:

Wood-wool:

Wood-wool is made by shaving wood. Use it to make a firm foundation for head or body, pushing the stuffing in with a big screwdriver.

Polyester fiberfill:

This material has resilience and is easy to handle. Use polyester fiberfill for stuffing body, arms, and legs as well as for shaping crown of hat.

Cotton jersey:

Jersey is an elastic fabric often used for underclothes. Choose a lightweight apricot pink for doll making. You can also dye a white T-shirt in hot water with 2 tea bags. Remove shirt when it has the desired color. Use white rayon to line arms and legs to prevent them from stretching.

Cotton:

Cotton helps to make a smooth face. Don't cut the cotton with scissors but tear pieces off by hand in order to overlap ends smoothly. Cotton 0.5 cm thick is a good size to work with.

Fabrics for dress:

Cotton prints and solids, denim, terry cloth, corduroy, quilted fabric, felt, lace, and cotton gloves are all usable, but avoid heavyweight or easily raveled fabrics. Small designs in subdued colors are more suitable for dolls than big designs in vivid colors.

White rayon:

This is used for lining body, arms, and legs. It is thicker than ordinary lining and slippery, but it helps prevent jersey from stretching and makes stuffing easier. You can use lightweight cotton as a substitute.

Screwdriver:

Screwdrivers are very useful tools. A bit one, about 13 cm long excluding handle and 0.5 cm wide, is used for pushing wood-wool. A small one, about 0.3 cm wide, is used for turning things inside out or stuffing small areas.

Materials for hair:

In general, yarn is used for hair. There are several kinds: 3-ply or baby yarn, mohair, looped yarn, and so on. Embroidery cotton No. 8 is also used. Remember that the strands of yarn should be combed and the color should match the face and dress. Use the same yarn to sew the hair on to doll's head.

Polyester georgette:

Georgette is used for eyes, but any lightweight fabric with horizontal threads that can be easily drawn is good. It is important to cut eyes out carefully using sharp scissors. Otherwise they will be angled.

Lace edging:

Use cotton and polyester lace edgings. Choose small designs and small scallops. You can save time if you use gathered edgings. Dye lace to match dress if you cannot find the color you need.

OTHER MATERIALS AND TOOLS:

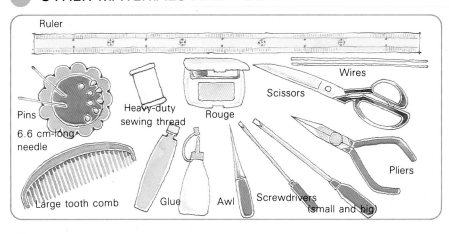

Ruler

Pins

6.6 cm-long needle

Heavy-duty sewing thread

Rouge

Large tooth comb

Glue

Awl

Screwdrivers (small and big)

Scissors

Wires

Pliers

Use scissors with sharp points and a glue that dries clear—glue is used to attach the nose and eyes, and also holds ribbon bows and artificial flowers in place.

Use 6.6 cm-long needle for sewing body and embroidering mouth. Use an ordinary sewing needle for making dresses, stitching body and so on.

Use a large-tooth comb made of wood for yarn hair.

Key for doll making:

When you are making the foundation think of a healthy body shape, and think of the character of your doll when making its features. Even dolls made with the same pattern will look different when made by different people, and the measurements are only a guide—create your own doll by changing them. Just remember that the foundation is very important, although it cannot be seen, so make it carefully.

Choose any color you like, but keep in mind that too many colors will spoil attractiveness of your doll. Make the best use of soft colors and create tasteful styles. The most important thing is to keep your hands working and enjoy the doll you are making.

How to make features:

Eyes: Using sharp scissors and cutting with the grain, cut out teardrop shapes for eyes.

Mouth: Embroider mouth with six-strand embroidery floss, No. 25, pulling thread a little to purse up. Use long needle.

Freckles: Dot freckles with felt-tipped pen in brown. Carefully make small dots.

Girl: Space between eyes should be wider than that of boy, but narrower than that of baby. Make small nose and mouth.

Aged people:

Make small eyes and glue on diagonally as shown. Embroider wrinkles with one strand of heavy-duty sewing thread.

Baby: Make big eyes, placing them well apart, and glue onto face. Glue nose between eyes. Make small nose and mouth.

Boy: Place eyes close to each other. Make bigger nose and mouth.

Clown:

Make big nose. Place eyes and nose close to each other. Embroider on a big mouth. Rub rouge on nose.

MATERIALS:
For face: See page 69. For body, arms, and legs: White rayon, 65 cm by 25 cm. For arms and legs: Cotton jersey, 45 cm by 25 cm. For hat, dress, pantalettes, and shoes: Unbleached sheeting, 90 cm by 57 cm. For hair: Jute. For stuffing: Wood-wool; cotton; polyester fiberfill.
FINISHED SIZE: 42 cm tall.
DIRECTIONS:
Make face following instructions on pages 69–73. Stuff body firmly with wood-wool, hands and feet with polyester fiberfill, and arms and legs with rolled-up cotton. Follow illustrated instructions for dressing. Make features and attach hair.

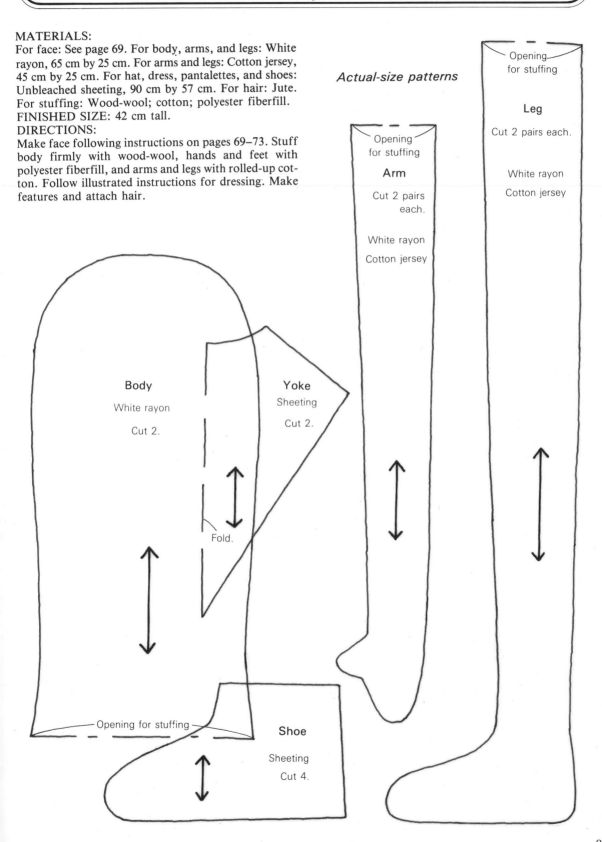

Actual-size patterns

Opening for stuffing

Leg

Cut 2 pairs each.

White rayon

Cotton jersey

Opening for stuffing

Arm

Cut 2 pairs each.

White rayon

Cotton jersey

Body

White rayon

Cut 2.

Yoke

Sheeting

Cut 2.

Fold.

Opening for stuffing

Shoe

Sheeting

Cut 4.

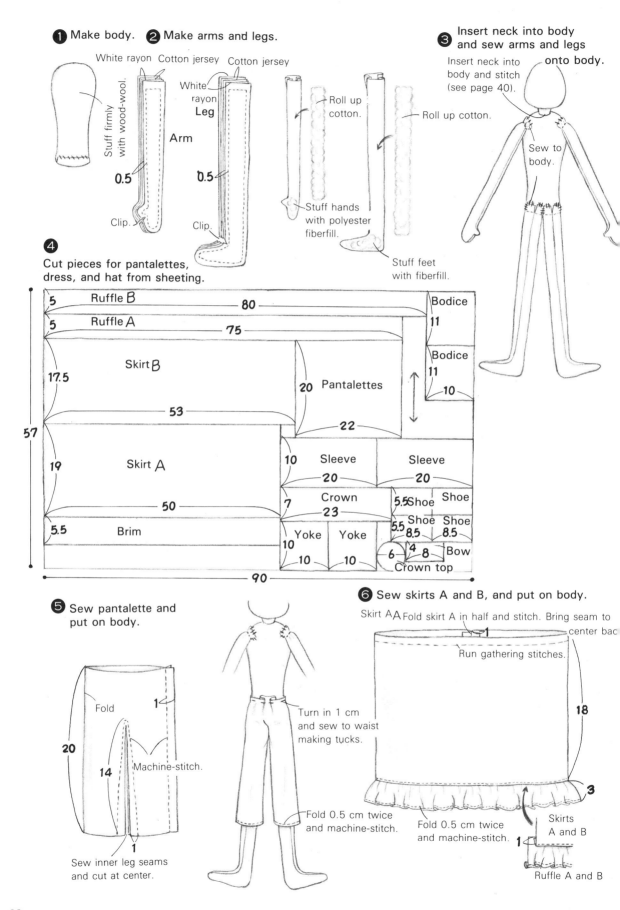

1 Make body. **2** Make arms and legs.

3 Insert neck into body and sew arms and legs **onto body.**

White rayon   Cotton jersey   Cotton jersey

White rayon

Stuff firmly with wood-wool.

Arm   Leg

0.5   0.5

Clip.   Clip.

Roll up cotton.

Roll up cotton.

Stuff hands with polyester fiberfill.

Stuff feet with fiberfill.

Insert neck into body and stitch (see page 40).

Sew to body.

4 Cut pieces for pantalettes, dress, and hat from sheeting.

Ruffle B — 5 — 80 — Bodice
Ruffle A — 5 — 75 — 11
Skirt B — 17.5 — 20 Pantalettes — Bodice 11
57 — 53 — 22 — 10
Skirt A — 19 — 10 Sleeve — 20   Sleeve — 20
50 — 7 Crown — 23   5.5 Shoe   Shoe
Brim — 5.5 — Yoke   Yoke   5.5 Shoe   Shoe
10 — 10   10   6   4   8   Bow   8.5   8.5
90 — Crown top

5 Sew pantalette and put on body.

Fold   1
20   14   Machine-stitch.
Sew inner leg seams and cut at center.

Turn in 1 cm and sew to waist making tucks.

Fold 0.5 cm twice and machine-stitch.

6 Sew skirts A and B, and put on body.

Skirt A   Fold skirt A in half and stitch. Bring seam to center back.
Run gathering stitches.
18
3
Fold 0.5 cm twice and machine-stitch.   Skirts A and B
1   Ruffle A and B

7 Sew sleeves and put on body.

Sew onto body.

Pull up gathers.

End of stitching

Run gathering stitches.

10

2

1

1

Turn in seam allowance and pull up gathers.

Pin tuck

0.1

Skirt B

Pull up gathers and sew onto waist.

1

1

Skirt A

0.7

2

8 Put on bodice.

Back

Slip-stitch.

Turn in 1 cm and glue.

9 Place yoke.

Turn in 1 cm and machine-stitch.

Turn in extra fabric around neck.

Sew shoulder seams.

Fold front edges as shown and glue onto body.

Back

10 Glue bow.

6

2

Fold 0.5 cm twice and machine-stitch.

Run gathering stitches at center.

Pull up gathers, fold as shown and sew onto yoke.

11 Put on shoes.

Turn in 1 cm.

Insert foot into shoe.

Slip-stitch.

Machine-stitch.

12 Attach hair.

Place 30 strands of jute on head and sew onto head taking a long stitch at center.

35

30 strands of jute

Untwist jute into 3 ply.

13 Make hat.

Crown top

4

Pull up gathers.

Crown

5

Brim

3.5

Fold 0.5 cm twice and machine-stitch.

FINISHED DIAGRAM

Nose   Eye

0.7

0.4   0.4

Glue nose and eyes in place.

Rub rouge

Embroider mouth.

42

Debutantes, shown on pages 2 & 3.

MATERIALS:

For face: See page 69.

[For each doll] For body and sleeves: Polyester lace and quilted satin, 90 cm by 50 cm each; felt and cardboard, 8 cm square each; wood-wool; weight for bottom. For hands: White rayon and cotton jersey, 10 cm square each. For hair: Mohair yarn.

[For Doll A (right, page 3)]: Lace edging, 2 cm by 150 cm; braid, 0.7 cm by 500 cm; 10 ready-made appliqués; artificial flowers. [For Doll B (left, page 3)] Ruffled lace, 3.5 cm by 215 cm; ribbon, 3.8 cm by 100 cm; braid, 0.7 cm by 10 cm; artificial flowers.

[For Doll C (right, page 2)] Ruffled lace edging, 3.5 cm by 210 cm; ribbon, 2.8 cm by 80 cm; braid, 0.7 cm by 10 cm; one button, 1 cm in diameter; artificial flowers.

[For Doll D (left, page 3)] Braid, 1.8 cm by 200 cm; braid, 0.7 cm by 10 cm; flower-shaped braid, 0.6 cm by 5 cm; artificial flowers.

FINISHED SIZE: 48 cm tall.

DIRECTIONS:

Make face following instructions on pages 69–73. Make smaller face. Stuff body firmly with wood-wool and put weight at bottom. Sew ends of braid or lace edging but glue other parts.

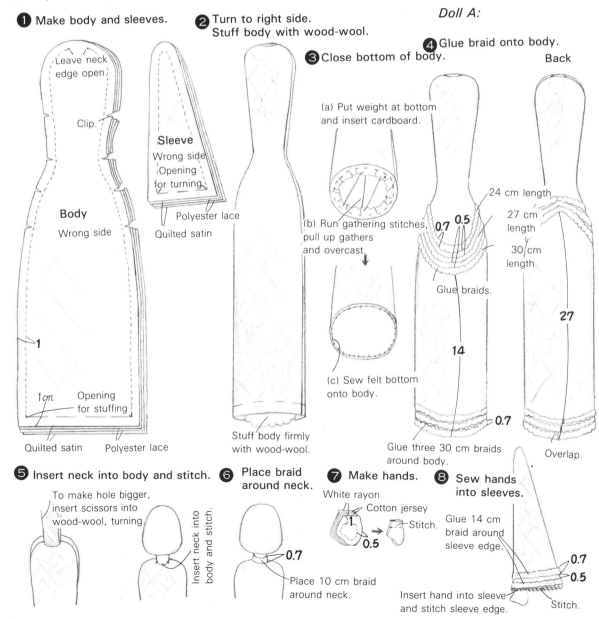

1 Make body and sleeves.

2 Turn to right side. Stuff body with wood-wool.

Doll A:

3 Close bottom of body.

4 Glue braid onto body.

Leave neck edge open.

Clip.

Sleeve
Wrong side
Opening for turning
Polyester lace
Quilted satin

Body
Wrong side

1

1 cm   Opening for stuffing

Quilted satin   Polyester lace

Stuff body firmly with wood-wool.

(a) Put weight at bottom and insert cardboard.

(b) Run gathering stitches, pull up gathers and overcast.

(c) Sew felt bottom onto body.

Back

24 cm length
27 cm length
30 cm length

0.7 0.5

Glue braids.

14

0.7

Glue three 30 cm braids around body.

27

Overlap.

5 Insert neck into body and stitch.

To make hole bigger, insert scissors into wood-wool, turning.

Insert neck into body and stitch.

6 Place braid around neck.

0.7

Place 10 cm braid around neck.

7 Make hands.

White rayon
Cotton jersey
Stitch.
0.5

8 Sew hands into sleeves.

Glue 14 cm braid around sleeve edge.

0.7
0.5

Insert hand into sleeve and stitch sleeve edge.

Stitch.

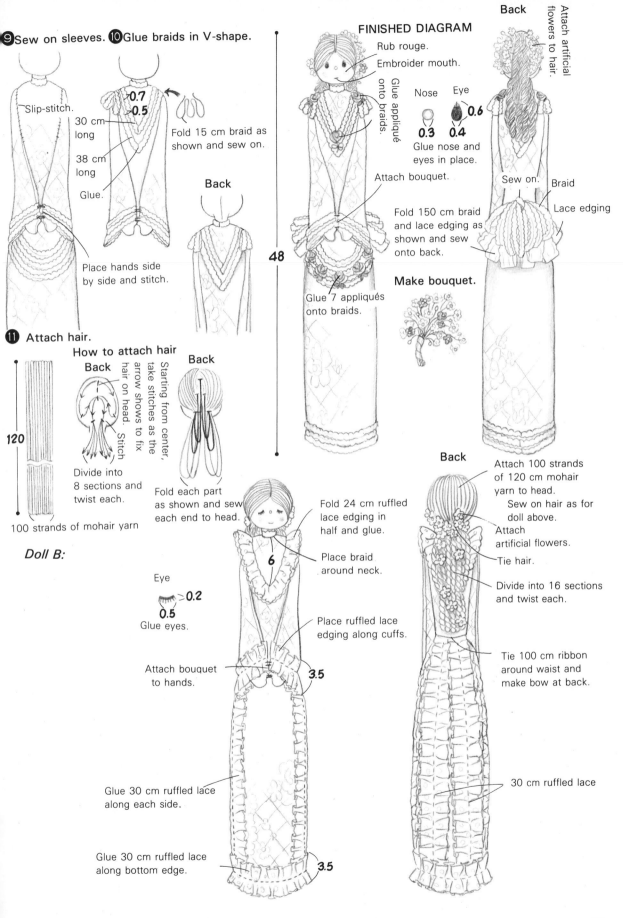

9 Sew on sleeves. **10** Glue braids in V-shape.

Slip-stitch.

0.7
0.5

30 cm long

38 cm long

Glue.

Fold 15 cm braid as shown and sew on.

Place hands side by side and stitch.

Back

FINISHED DIAGRAM

Rub rouge.

Embroider mouth.

Rub rouge.

Glue appliqué onto braids.

Nose

Eye

0.6

0.3 0.4

Glue nose and eyes in place.

Attach bouquet.

Fold 150 cm braid and lace edging as shown and sew onto back.

Glue 7 appliqués onto braids.

48

Back

Attach artificial flowers to hair.

Sew on. Braid

Lace edging

Make bouquet.

11 Attach hair.

How to attach hair

Back

Starting from center, take stitches as the arrow shows to fix hair on head. Stitch

Divide into 8 sections and twist each.

Back

Fold each part as shown and sew each end to head.

120

100 strands of mohair yarn

Doll B:

Eye

0.2

0.5

Glue eyes.

Fold 24 cm ruffled lace edging in half and glue.

Place braid around neck.

Place ruffled lace edging along cuffs.

6

Attach bouquet to hands.

3.5

Glue 30 cm ruffled lace along each side.

Glue 30 cm ruffled lace along bottom edge.

3.5

Back

Attach 100 strands of 120 cm mohair yarn to head.

Sew on hair as for doll above.

Attach artificial flowers.

Tie hair.

Divide into 16 sections and twist each.

Tie 100 cm ribbon around waist and make bow at back.

30 cm ruffled lace

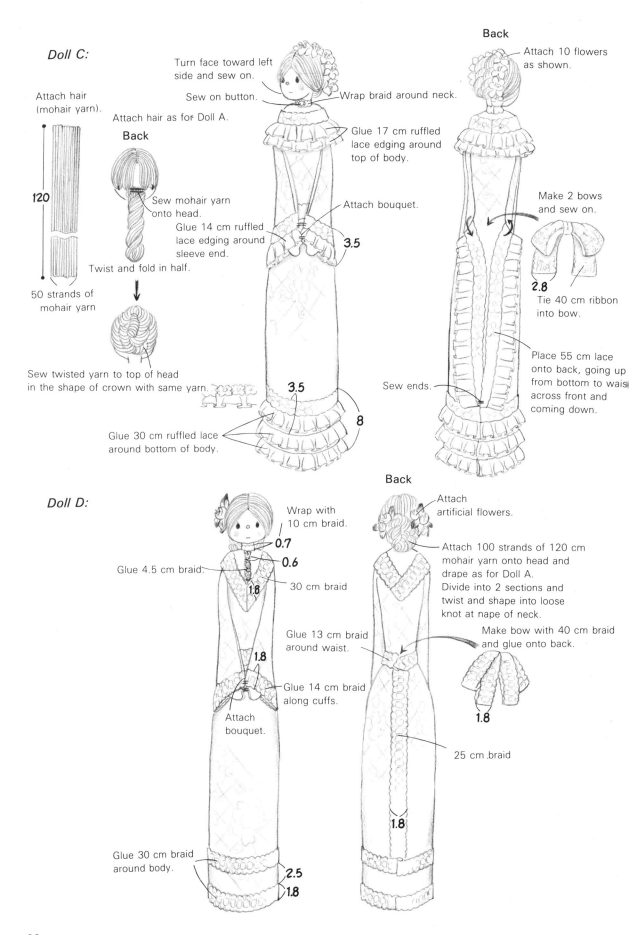

Doll C:

Attach hair
(mohair yarn).

120

50 strands of
mohair yarn

Back

Sew mohair yarn
onto head.

Twist and fold in half.

Sew twisted yarn to top of head
in the shape of crown with same yarn.

Turn face toward left
side and sew on.

Sew on button.

Attach hair as for Doll A.

Wrap braid around neck.

Glue 17 cm ruffled
lace edging around
top of body.

Attach bouquet.

Glue 14 cm ruffled
lace edging around
sleeve end.

3.5

3.5

8

Glue 30 cm ruffled lace
around bottom of body.

Back

Attach 10 flowers
as shown.

Make 2 bows
and sew on.

2.8

Tie 40 cm ribbon
into bow.

Sew ends.

Place 55 cm lace
onto back, going up
from bottom to wais
across front and
coming down.

Doll D:

Wrap with
10 cm braid.

0.7

0.6

Glue 4.5 cm braid.

1.8

30 cm braid

1.8

Glue 13 cm braid
around waist.

Glue 14 cm braid
along cuffs.

Attach
bouquet.

Glue 30 cm braid
around body.

2.5

1.8

Back

Attach
artificial flowers.

Attach 100 strands of 120 cm
mohair yarn onto head and
drape as for Doll A.
Divide into 2 sections and
twist and shape into loose
knot at nape of neck.

Make bow with 40 cm braid
and glue onto back.

1.8

25 cm .braid

1.8

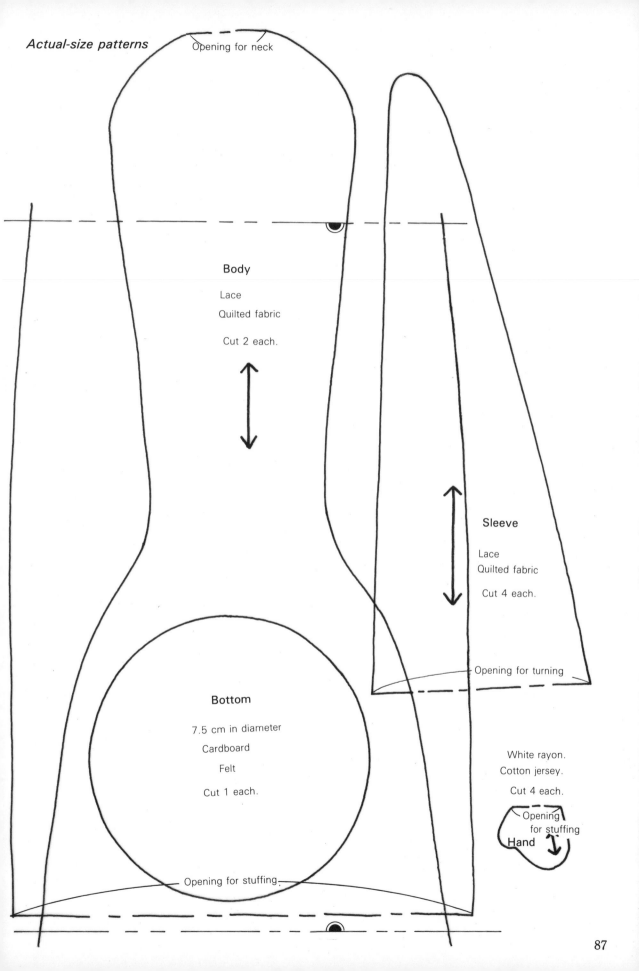

Actual-size patterns

Opening for neck

Body

Lace

Quilted fabric

Cut 2 each.

Sleeve

Lace
Quilted fabric

Cut 4 each.

Opening for turning

Bottom

7.5 cm in diameter

Cardboard

Felt

Cut 1 each.

White rayon.
Cotton jersey.

Cut 4 each.

Opening
for stuffing

Hand

Opening for stuffing

Friends, shown on pages 4 & 5.

MATERIALS:

For face: See page 69.

[For each doll] For body, arms, and legs: White rayon, 55 cm by 15 cm. For arms: Cotton jersey, 20 cm by 15 cm. For legs: Cotton stripes, 25 cm by 15 cm. For shoes: Felt, 10 cm by 5 cm. For stuffing: Wood-wool; cotton; polyester fiberfill; wire #16.

[For Boy] For clothes: Cotton fabric, 34 cm by 23 cm; lace edging, 3 cm by 30 cm; ribbon, 0.6 cm by 25 cm. For hair:Polyester cord, 100 cm.

[For Girl] For drawers and petticoat: White cotton broadcloth, 50 cm by 12 cm; cotton lace edging, 2.5 cm by 30 cm. For dress: Cotton print, 35 cm by 21 cm; lace edging, 2 cm by 70 cm; ribbon, 0.6 cm by 40 cm. For hair: Polyester cord, 125 cm. Artificial flowers.

FINISHED SIZE: See diagrams.

DIRECTIONS:

Make face following instructions on pages 69–73. Stuff body firmly with wood-wool, hands and feet with fiberfill, and arms and legs with rolled cotton. Assemble body and put on clothes following individual instructions. Bend arms and legs as shown.

Boy:

❶ Make body.

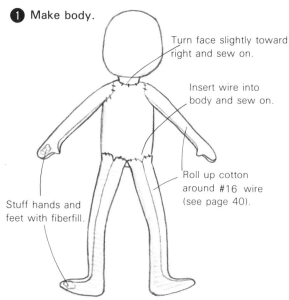

Turn face slightly toward right and sew on.

Insert wire into body and sew on.

Roll up cotton around #16 wire (see page 40).

Stuff hands and feet with fiberfill.

❷ Cut out pieces for top and pants from cotton fabric.

❸ Sew pants and put on body.

Actual-size patterns

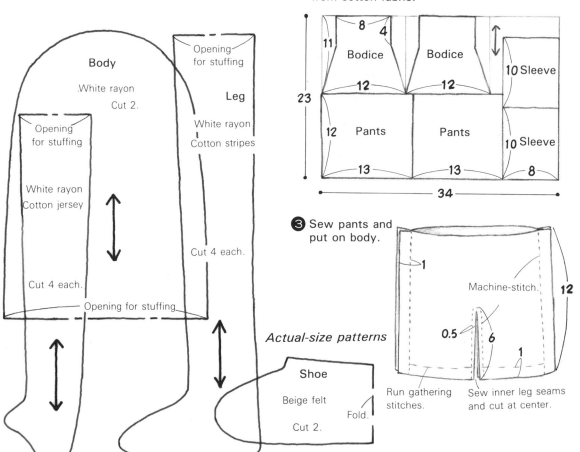

Body
White rayon
Cut 2.

Opening for stuffing

Opening for stuffing

White rayon
Cotton jersey

Cut 4 each.

Opening for stuffing

Leg

White rayon
Cotton stripes

Cut 4 each.

Opening for stuffing

Shoe
Beige felt
Cut 2.
Fold.

Bodice Bodice
8 4
11
12 12
23
12 Pants Pants
13 13
10 Sleeve
10 Sleeve
8
34

Machine-stitch.
1
12
0.5 6
1
Run gathering stitches.
Sew inner leg seams and cut at center.

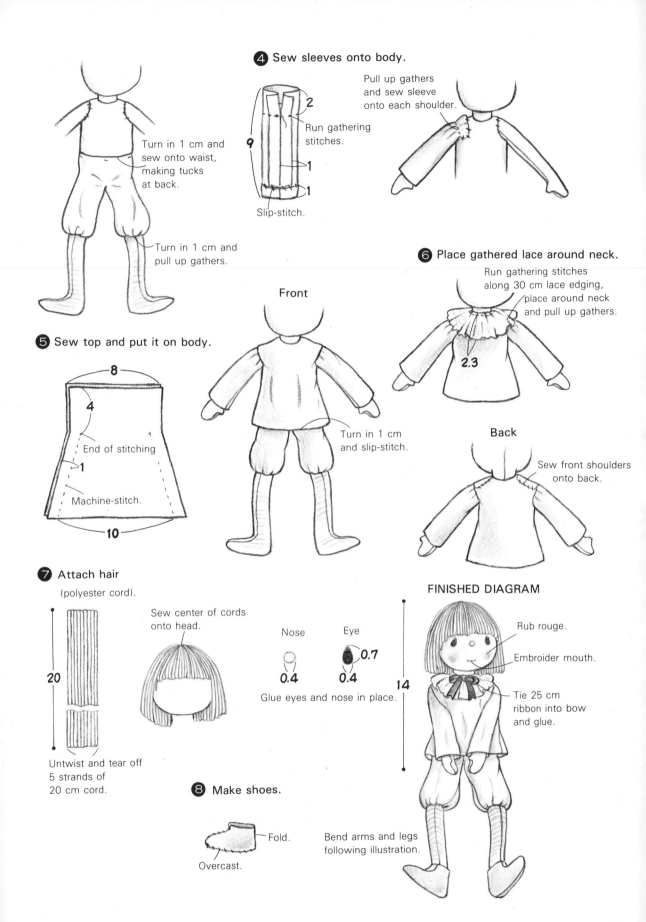

④ Sew sleeves onto body.

Turn in 1 cm and sew onto waist, making tucks at back.

Turn in 1 cm and pull up gathers.

Run gathering stitches.

2

9

1

1

Slip-stitch.

Pull up gathers and sew sleeve onto each shoulder.

⑥ Place gathered lace around neck.

Run gathering stitches along 30 cm lace edging, place around neck and pull up gathers.

2.3

⑤ Sew top and put it on body.

8

4

End of stitching

1

Machine-stitch.

10

Front

Turn in 1 cm and slip-stitch.

Back

Sew front shoulders onto back.

⑦ Attach hair

(polyester cord).

Sew center of cords onto head.

20

Untwist and tear off 5 strands of 20 cm cord.

Nose

0.4

Eye

0.7

0.4

Glue eyes and nose in place.

FINISHED DIAGRAM

Rub rouge.

Embroider mouth.

14

Tie 25 cm ribbon into bow and glue.

⑧ Make shoes.

Fold.

Overcast.

Bend arms and legs following illustration.

Girl:

1 Make body.

Turn face toward left and stitch.

2 Cut out pieces for drawers and petticoat from cotton broadcloth.

12

Drawers

8

Petticoat

20

30

50

3 Sew drawers and attach to body.

Fold.

Machine-stitch.

12

6

0.5

1

1

Sew inner leg seams and cut at center.

Run gathering stitches.

Turn in 1 cm and sew around waist making tucks at back.

Turn in seam allowance and pull up gathers.

4 Sew petticoat and attach to body.

Turn in 1 cm, run gathering stitches and pull up gathers.

1.8

Lace edging

1

Lace edging 1.8

5 Cut out pieces for dress from print.

11

Sleeve

Sleeve

8

Bodice

Bodice

21

8

8

9

9

10

Skirt

35

6 Sew skirt and attach to body.

Press seam open.

1

Run gathering stitches.

1

9

1.5

Gather 50 cm lace edging and sew onto bottom edge.

Pull up gathers and sew onto body.

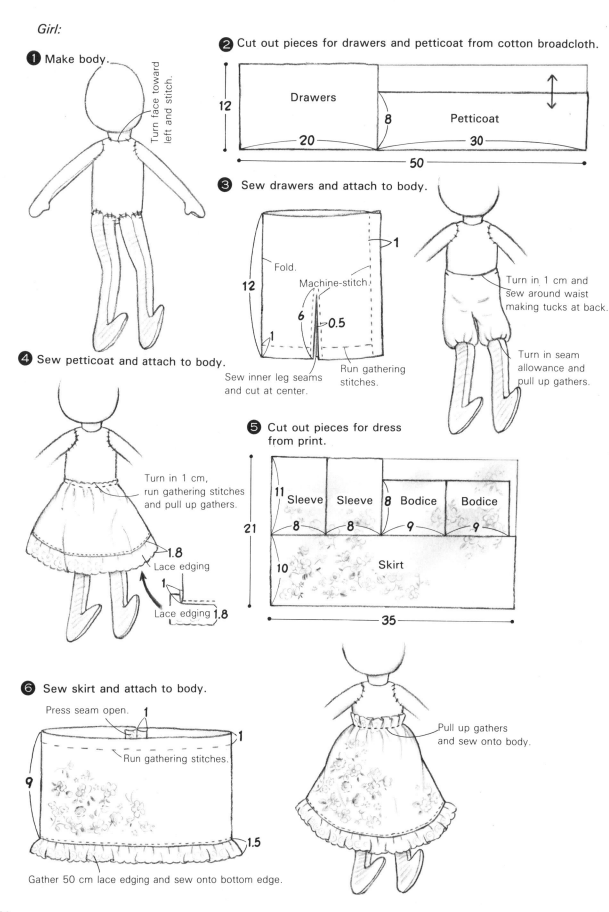

7 Sew sleeves.

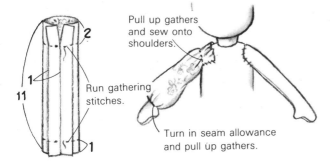

2

1

11

1

Run gathering stitches.

Pull up gathers and sew onto shoulders.

Turn in seam allowance and pull up gathers.

8 Sew on bodice.

Turn in 1 cm and glue.

9 Place collar around neck.

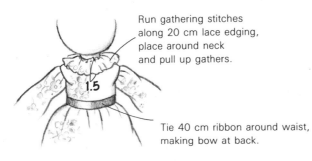

1.5

Run gathering stitches along 20 cm lace edging, place around neck and pull up gathers.

Tie 40 cm ribbon around waist, making bow at back.

Back

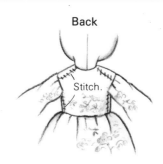

Stitch.

10 Attach hair.

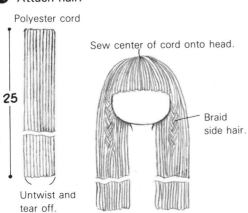

Polyester cord

25

Untwist and tear off.

Sew center of cord onto head.

Braid side hair.

FINISHED DIAGRAM

14

Make nose and eyes same size as for Boy.

Attach bouquet.

Bend arms.

Bouquet

Bonneted Girls, shown on pages 6 & 7.

MATERIALS:

For face: See page 69.

[For each doll] For body, arms, and legs: White rayon, 60 cm by 15 cm. For arms and legs: Cotton jersey, 40 cm by 15 cm. For drawers and petticoat: White cotton broadcloth, 48 cm by 10 cm; white cotton lace edging, 2.5 cm by 28 cm. For bonnet: Iron-on interfacing, 18 cm by 10 cm. For shoes: Felt, 10 cm by 6 cm. For hair: Bouclé yarn. For stuffing: Wood-wool; cotton; polyester fiberfill.

[For Doll at Left] Cotton print, 84 cm by 22cm; cotton lace edging, 2.5 cm by 100 cm; ribbon, 0.7 cm by 90 cm.

[For Doll at Center] Cotton print, 75 cm by 22 cm; braid, 0.5 cm by 115 cm; ruffled lace edging, 4 cm by 80 cm; ribbon 0.7 cm by 40 cm.

[For Doll at Right] Cotton stripe, 84 cm by 26 cm; scrap of white cotton broadcloth; lace edging, 1 cm by 140 cm; ribbon, 0.7 cm by 40 cm.

FINISHED SIZE: 24 cm tall.

DIRECTIONS:

Make face following instructions on pages 69–73. Stuff body firmly with wood-wool, hands and feet with fiberfill and arms and legs with rolled cotton. Assemble body and put on clothes.

Actual-size patterns

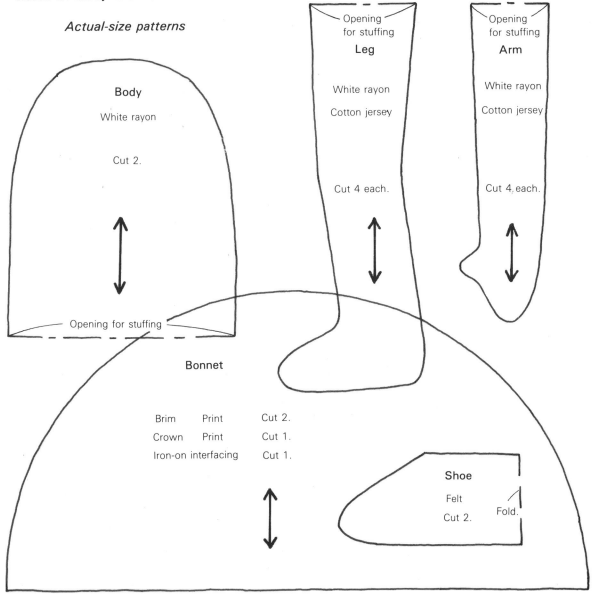

Body
White rayon
Cut 2.
Opening for stuffing

Opening for stuffing
Leg
White rayon
Cotton jersey
Cut 4 each.

Opening for stuffing
Arm
White rayon
Cotton jersey
Cut 4 each.

Bonnet

Brim	Print	Cut 2.
Crown	Print	Cut 1.
Iron-on interfacing		Cut 1.

Shoe
Felt
Cut 2.
Fold.

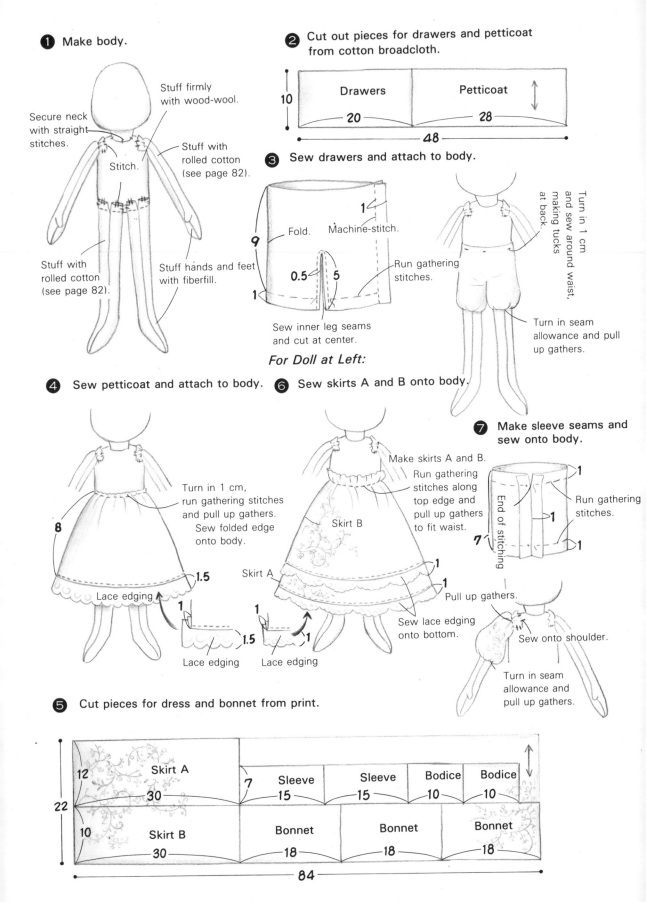

1 Make body.

Stuff firmly with wood-wool.

Secure neck with straight stitches.

Stitch.

Stuff with rolled cotton (see page 82).

Stuff with rolled cotton (see page 82).

Stuff hands and feet with fiberfill.

2 Cut out pieces for drawers and petticoat from cotton broadcloth.

10

Drawers
20

Petticoat
28

48

3 Sew drawers and attach to body.

9

Fold.

1

Machine-stitch.

0.5 5

1

Run gathering stitches.

Sew inner leg seams and cut at center.

Turn in 1 cm and sew around waist, making tucks at back.

Turn in seam allowance and pull up gathers.

For Doll at Left:

4 Sew petticoat and attach to body.

6 Sew skirts A and B onto body.

8

Turn in 1 cm, run gathering stitches and pull up gathers. Sew folded edge onto body.

1.5

Lace edging

1

1.5

Lace edging

Make skirts A and B. Run gathering stitches along top edge and pull up gathers to fit waist.

Skirt B

Skirt A

1

1

Pull up gathers.

Sew lace edging onto bottom.

1

Lace edging

7 Make sleeve seams and sew onto body.

1

Run gathering stitches.

1

7

End of stitching

Sew onto shoulder.

Turn in seam allowance and pull up gathers.

5 Cut pieces for dress and bonnet from print.

12

Skirt A
30

7

Sleeve
15

Sleeve
15

Bodice
10

Bodice
10

22

10

Skirt B
30

Bonnet
18

Bonnet
18

Bonnet
18

84

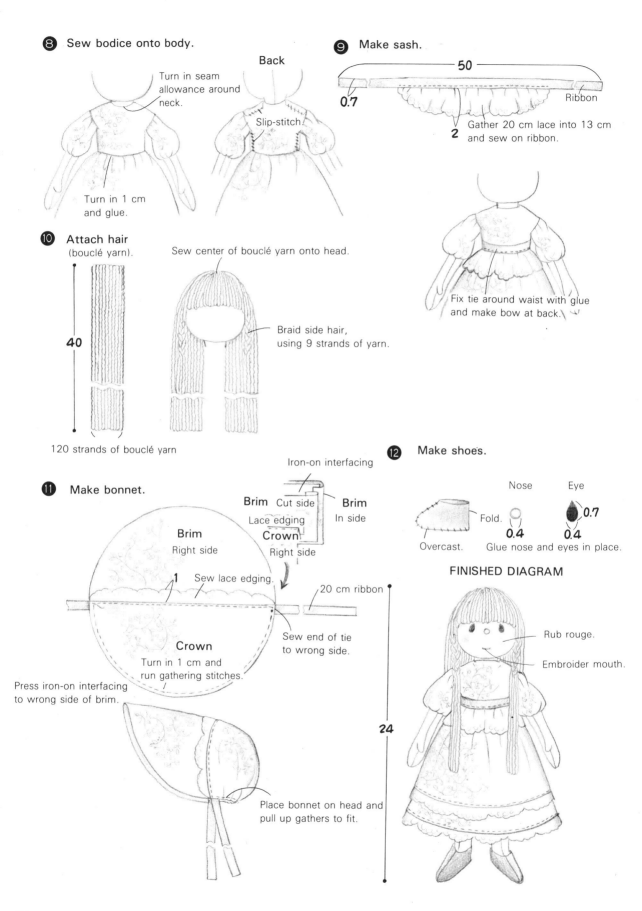

8 Sew bodice onto body.

Turn in seam allowance around neck.

Back

Slip-stitch.

Turn in 1 cm and glue.

9 Make sash.

50

0.7

Ribbon

2

Gather 20 cm lace into 13 cm and sew on ribbon.

Fix tie around waist with glue and make bow at back.

10 Attach hair (bouclé yarn).

Sew center of bouclé yarn onto head.

40

Braid side hair, using 9 strands of yarn.

120 strands of bouclé yarn

11 Make bonnet.

Iron-on interfacing

Brim
Cut side

Brim
In side

Crown
Right side

Brim
Right side

1 Sew lace edging.

20 cm ribbon

Sew end of tie to wrong side.

Crown

Turn in 1 cm and run gathering stitches.

Press iron-on interfacing to wrong side of brim.

Place bonnet on head and pull up gathers to fit.

12 Make shoes.

Fold.

Overcast.

Nose

0.4

Eye

0.7

0.4

Glue nose and eyes in place.

FINISHED DIAGRAM

Rub rouge.

Embroider mouth.

24

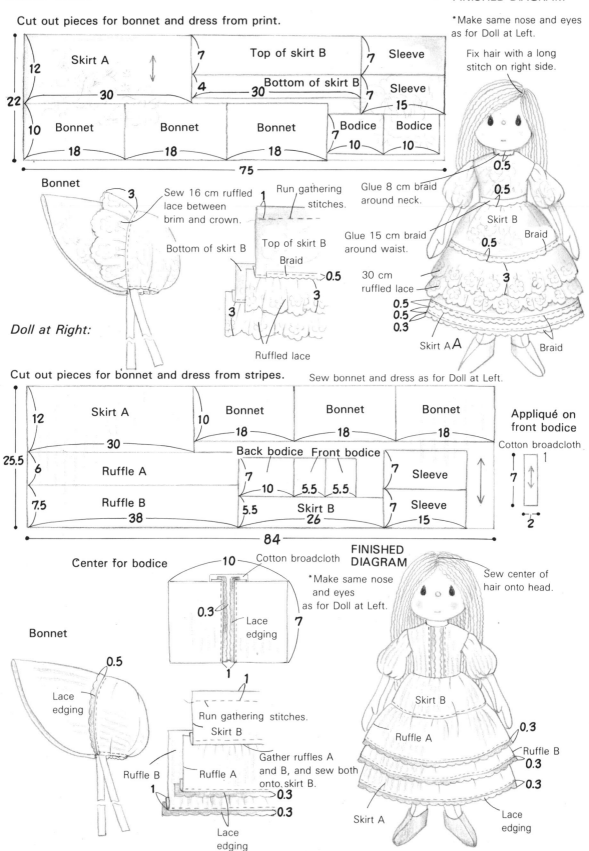

Doll at Center:

Cut out pieces for bonnet and dress from print.

Skirt A

12

22

7 Top of skirt B

7 Sleeve

4 Bottom of skirt B

30 30

7 Sleeve

10

Bonnet Bonnet Bonnet

7 Bodice Bodice

15

18 18 18

7 10 10

75

FINISHED DIAGRAM

*Make same nose and eyes as for Doll at Left.

Fix hair with a long stitch on right side.

0.5

0.5

Skirt B

Braid

0.5

3

30 cm ruffled lace

0.5
0.5
0.3

Skirt A A

Braid

Glue 8 cm braid around neck.

Glue 15 cm braid around waist.

Bonnet

3

Sew 16 cm ruffled lace between brim and crown.

Bottom of skirt B

Top of skirt B

Braid

1 Run gathering stitches.

0.5

3

3

Ruffled lace

Doll at Right:

Cut out pieces for bonnet and dress from stripes.

Sew bonnet and dress as for Doll at Left.

Skirt A

12

25.5

10

Bonnet Bonnet Bonnet

18 18 18

30

6 Ruffle A

Back bodice Front bodice

7 7 Sleeve

10 5.5 5.5

7.5 Ruffle B

5.5 Skirt B

7 Sleeve

38 26 15

84

Appliqué on front bodice

Cotton broadcloth

1

7

2

FINISHED DIAGRAM

*Make same nose and eyes as for Doll at Left.

Sew center of hair onto head.

Center for bodice

10 Cotton broadcloth

0.3 Lace edging

7

1 1

Bonnet

0.5

Lace edging

Run gathering stitches.

Skirt B

Ruffle B Ruffle A

Gather ruffles A and B, and sew both onto skirt B.

1

0.3
0.3

Lace edging

Skirt B

0.3

Ruffle A

Ruffle B

0.3

0.3

Skirt A

Lace edging

Country Girl, shown on pages 8 & 9.

MATERIALS:
For face: See page 69. For body, arms, and legs: White rayon, 60 cm by 35 cm. For arms and legs: Cotton jersey, 60 cm by 35 cm. For drawers and petticoat: White cotton broadcloth, 68 cm by 25 cm; ruffled lace edging, 4 cm by 43 cm. For hat and dress: Gingham checks, 79 cm by 28 cm; cotton lace, 20 cm by 113 cm; ruffled lace edging, 4 cm by 100 cm; ribbon, 0.6 cm by 40 cm; 3 buttons, 0.4 cm in diameter. For hair: Looped yarn. For stuffing: Cardboard; wood-wool; cotton; polyester fiberfill.

FINISHED SIZE: 53 cm tall.
DIRECTIONS:
Make face following instructions on pages 69–73. Stuff body firmly with wood-wool, hands and feet with fiberfill, and arms and legs with rolled cotton. Assemble body and put on dress. Attach hair and make features.

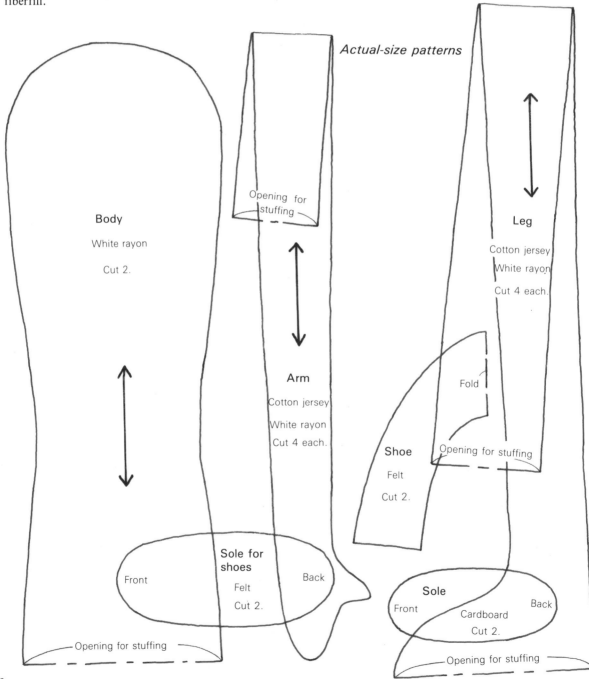

Actual-size patterns

Body
White rayon
Cut 2.

Opening for stuffing

Arm
Cotton jersey
White rayon
Cut 4 each.

Leg
Cotton jersey
White rayon
Cut 4 each.

Fold

Opening for stuffing

Shoe
Felt
Cut 2.

Sole for shoes
Felt
Cut 2.

Front

Back

Sole
Cardboard
Cut 2.

Front

Back

Opening for stuffing

Opening for stuffing

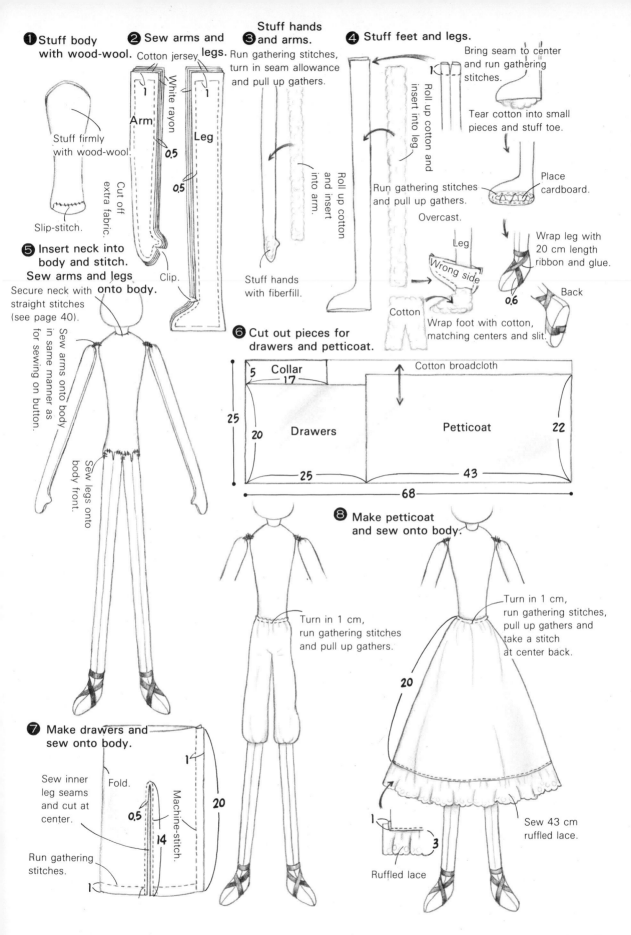

❶ Stuff body with wood-wool.

Stuff firmly with wood-wool.

Slip-stitch.

❷ Sew arms and legs.

Cotton jersey

White rayon

Arm

Leg

1

1

0.5

0.5

Cut off extra fabric.

Clip.

❸ Stuff hands and arms.

Run gathering stitches, turn in seam allowance and pull up gathers.

Roll up cotton and insert into arm.

Stuff hands with fiberfill.

❹ Stuff feet and legs.

Roll up cotton and insert into leg

1

Bring seam to center and run gathering stitches.

Tear cotton into small pieces and stuff toe.

Place cardboard.

Run gathering stitches and pull up gathers.

Overcast.

Leg

Wrong side

Cotton

Wrap foot with cotton, matching centers and slit.

Wrap leg with 20 cm length ribbon and glue.

0.6

Back

❺ Insert neck into body and stitch. Sew arms and legs onto body.

Secure neck with straight stitches (see page 40).

Sew arms onto body in same manner as for sewing on button.

Sew legs onto body front.

❻ Cut out pieces for drawers and petticoat.

Collar		Cotton broadcloth

5

17

25

20

Drawers

Petticoat

22

25

43

68

❼ Make drawers and sew onto body.

Sew inner leg seams and cut at center.

Run gathering stitches.

Fold.

Machine-stitch.

1

0.5

14

20

1

❽ Make petticoat and sew onto body.

Turn in 1 cm, run gathering stitches and pull up gathers.

Turn in 1 cm, run gathering stitches, pull up gathers and take a stitch at center back.

20

1

Sew 43 cm ruffled lace.

Ruffled lace

1

3

9 Cut out pieces for dress from gingham checks.

Skirt top
21
28
7
Skirt bottom
50

Bodice
14
Bodice 23
14
9

Sleeve Sleeve
10   10

79

Glue seam allowance.

Pull up gathers and take a stitch at center back.

10 Make skirt and sew onto body.

1 — Sew skirt into tube and press seam open.
1

20
Skirt top

5
Skirt bottom
3
3

Sew 50 cm ruffled lace.

1 — Skirt top
1 — Skirt bottom — Ruffled lace
3

12 Put on bodice.

11 Make sleeves and sew onto body.

2 — Pull up gathers.
Run gathering stitches
Stitch.
23   1
Press seam open.
Run gathering stitches
1

Turn in seam allowance and pull up gathers.

Back
Make a slit in neck at center back.

Make a diagonal slit in underarm at side.

Turn in 1 cm and glue.

Front

Stitch.

Back
Place front as for back and slip-stitch.

Slip-stitch.

Place collar around neck and sew ends.

Sew on buttons.

13 Sew collar.

Stitch three sides leaving center open.

Fold.
0.5
Fold.
Top-stitch.
2
Fold.
7.5

⓮ Cut out pieces for apron and hat from lace.

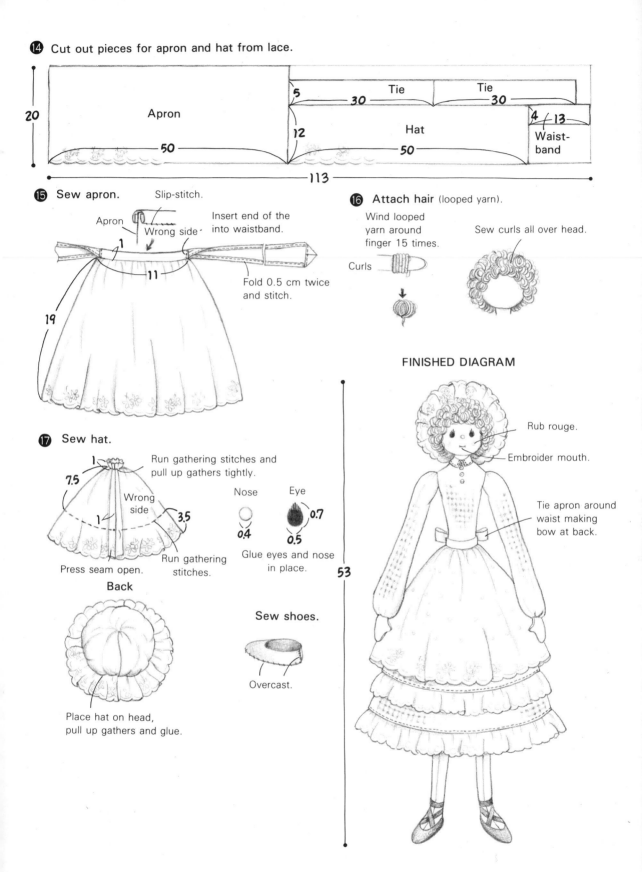

Apron		Tie	Tie

20

Apron

5

30   Tie   30   Tie

12

Hat

4 / 13

Waist-band

50

50

113

⓯ Sew apron.

Slip-stitch.

Apron

Wrong side

Insert end of the into waistband.

1

11

Fold 0.5 cm twice and stitch.

19

⓰ Attach hair (looped yarn).

Wind looped yarn around finger 15 times.

Sew curls all over head.

Curls

FINISHED DIAGRAM

⓱ Sew hat.

Run gathering stitches and pull up gathers tightly.

1

7.5

Wrong side

3.5

1

Run gathering stitches.

Press seam open.

Nose

0.4

Eye

0.7

0.5

Glue eyes and nose in place.

Back

Sew shoes.

Overcast.

Place hat on head, pull up gathers and glue.

Rub rouge.

Embroider mouth.

Tie apron around waist making bow at back.

53

Cute Memo Holders, shown on pages 10 & 11.

MATERIALS:

For face: See page 69.

[For A] Cotton print, 12 cm by 39 cm; quilted fabric, 12 cm by 38 cm; white cotton broadcloth, 18 cm square; lace edging, 3 cm by 70 cm; ribbon, 1.2 cm by 50 cm; 3 ready-made appliqués; looped yarn.

[For B] Cotton print, 23 cm by 45 cm; quilted fabric, 23 cm by 45 cm; gingham check, 18 cm square; braid, 0.7 cm by 80 cm; lace edging, 3 cm by 70 cm; one button, 1 cm in diameter; looped yarn.

[For C] Cotton print, 50 cm by 38 cm; quilted fabric, 15 cm by 32 cm; ribbon, 0.6 cm by 75 cm; mohair yarn; six-strand embroidery floss, No. 25 (pink, rose, brown, and gray).

[For D] Cotton print, 31 cm by 37 cm; quilted fabric, 20 cm by 37 cm; lace edging, 1.3 cm by 20 cm and 3 cm by 70 cm; ribbon, 0.6 cm by 60 cm; 4 ready-made appliqués; mohair yarn.

[For E] Cotton print, 29 cm by 35 cm; quilted fabric, 15 cm by 35 cm; pink cotton broadcloth, 18 cm square; lace edging, 3 cm by 70 cm; ribbon, 0.6 cm by 40 cm; Tyrolean tape, 2.5 cm by 13 cm; lace edging, 1.5 cm by 14 cm; polyester fiberfill; mohair yarn.

FINISHED SIZE: See diagrams.

DIRECTIONS:

Make face following instructions on pages 69–73. For Doll A: Sew body and attach head to body. Secure neck with straight stitches. Attach hair onto head. Put on hat and make features. Make Dolls B, C, and D as for Doll A. For Doll E: Make bodice with quilted fabric and attach head. Stuff bodice with fiberfill. Sew shirt (bag) and apron. Sew them onto bodice.

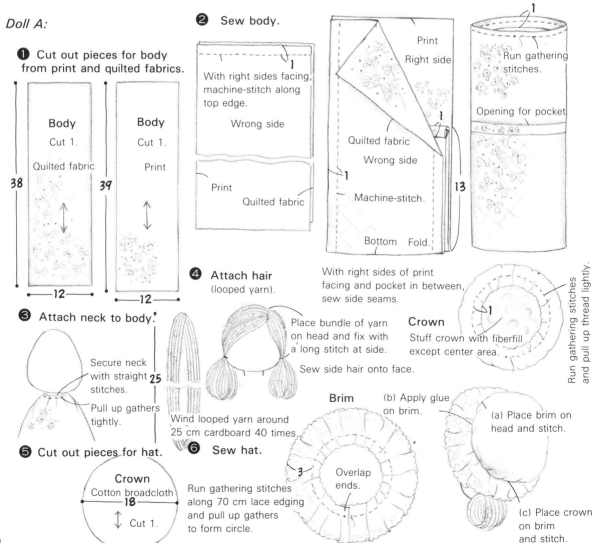

Doll A:

❶ Cut out pieces for body from print and quilted fabrics.

Body — Cut 1. — Quilted fabric — 38 — 12

Body — Cut 1. — Print — 39 — 12

❸ Attach neck to body.

Secure neck with straight stitches.
Pull up gathers tightly.

❺ Cut out pieces for hat.

Crown — Cotton broadcloth — 18 — Cut 1.

❷ Sew body.

With right sides facing, machine-stitch along top edge.
Wrong side
Print
Quilted fabric

Print — Right side
Quilted fabric — Wrong side
Machine-stitch.
Bottom — Fold.
13

With right sides of print facing and pocket in between, sew side seams.

❹ Attach hair (looped yarn).

Place bundle of yarn on head and fix with a long stitch at side.
Sew side hair onto face.

25

Wind looped yarn around 25 cm cardboard 40 times.

❻ Sew hat.

Run gathering stitches along 70 cm lace edging and pull up gathers to form circle.

Run gathering stitches.
Opening for pocket

Run gathering stitches and pull up thread lightly.

Crown
Stuff crown with fiberfill except center area.

Brim
Overlap ends.
3

(b) Apply glue on brim.
(a) Place brim on head and stitch.
(c) Place crown on brim and stitch.

100

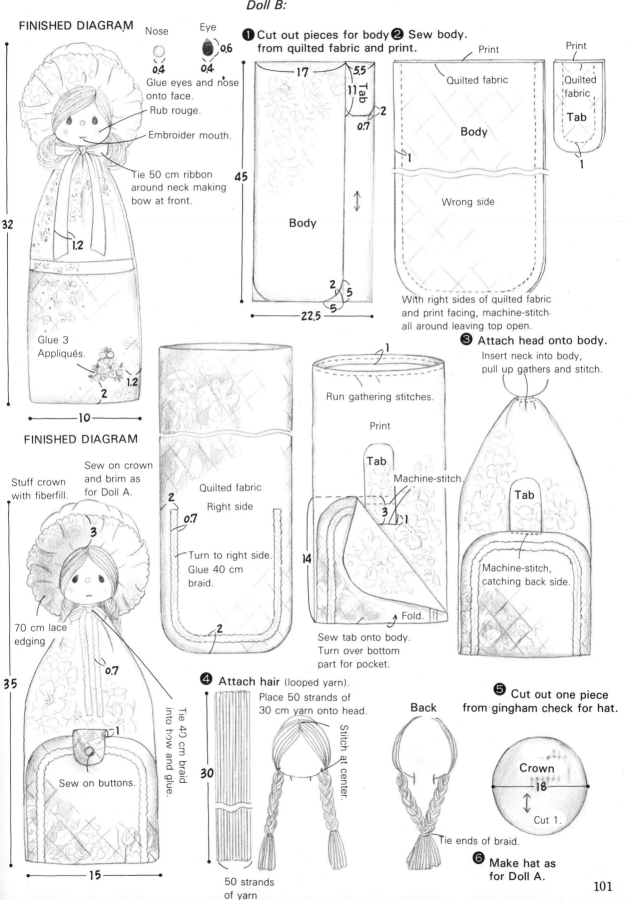

Doll B:

FINISHED DIAGRAM

Nose 0.4

Eye 0.6 0.4

Glue eyes and nose onto face.

Rub rouge.

Embroider mouth.

Tie 50 cm ribbon around neck making bow at front.

1.2

32

Glue 3 Appliqués.

2 1.2

10

❶ Cut out pieces for body from quilted fabric and print.

17 5.5

11 Tab

2

0.7

45

Body

22.5

2 5

5

❷ Sew body.

Print

Quilted fabric

Body

Wrong side

1

Print

Quilted fabric

Tab

1

With right sides of quilted fabric and print facing, machine-stitch all around leaving top open.

❸ Attach head onto body.

Insert neck into body, pull up gathers and stitch.

Run gathering stitches.

Print

Tab

Machine-stitch.

3 1

14

Fold.

Sew tab onto body. Turn over bottom part for pocket.

Tab

Machine-stitch, catching back side.

FINISHED DIAGRAM

Stuff crown with fiberfill.

Sew on crown and brim as for Doll A.

Quilted fabric

Right side

2

0.7

Turn to right side. Glue 40 cm braid.

70 cm lace edging

0.7

3

35

1

Tie 40 cm braid into bow and glue.

Sew on buttons.

2

15

❹ Attach hair (looped yarn).

Place 50 strands of 30 cm yarn onto head.

Stitch at center.

30

50 strands of yarn

Back

Tie ends of braid.

❺ Cut out one piece from gingham check for hat.

Crown

18

Cut 1.

❻ Make hat as for Doll A.

101

Doll C:

❶ Cut out pieces for hat and body.

Print

Body

15

38

32

Crown

18

6

Brim

50

Body

Quilted fabric

Cut 1.

32

15

Machine-stitch ribbon along pocket opening.

❷ Attach hair (mohair yarn).

How to attach hair

Place bundle of yarn on head and stitch at center and sides.

35

Tie with 20 cm ribbon.

Wind mohair yarn around 35 cm cardboard 50 times.

Doll D:

❶ Cut out pieces for hat and body from quilted fabric.

Pocket

8.5

7

Print

Body

Hat

18

37

Body

37

13

13

20

31

❷ Attach hair (mohair yarn).

Place bundle of yarn on head and stitch at center and sides.

35

4

Tie.

Tie with 20 cm ribbon.

Wind yarn around 35 cm cardboard 50 times.

FINISHED DIAGRAM

Brim

Fold.

2

1

Run gathering stitches.

Stuff crown with fiberfill.

Sew on crown and brim as for Doll A.

26

Opening for pocket

0.8

0.6

10

Turn in 1 cm, run gathering stitches and pull up gathers.

Tie 20 cm ribbon into bow and sew on.

Embroider.

13

Embroidery pattern (actual size)

Use 2 strands of floss unless otherwise indicated

Bullion rose (6 strands)

Darning

Lazy daisy

Outline

Satin

FINISHED DIAGRAM

Stuff crown with fiberfill.

3

Sew crown and brim as for Doll A.

70 cm lace edging

Turn in 1 cm; run gathering stitches, pull up gathers and stitch.

31

Opening for pocket

0.3

0.6

1

Glue appliqué.

Lace edging

Ribbon

0.3

0.6

1

12.5

6.5

2.5

5

2.5

1.5

Sew pocket onto body.

10

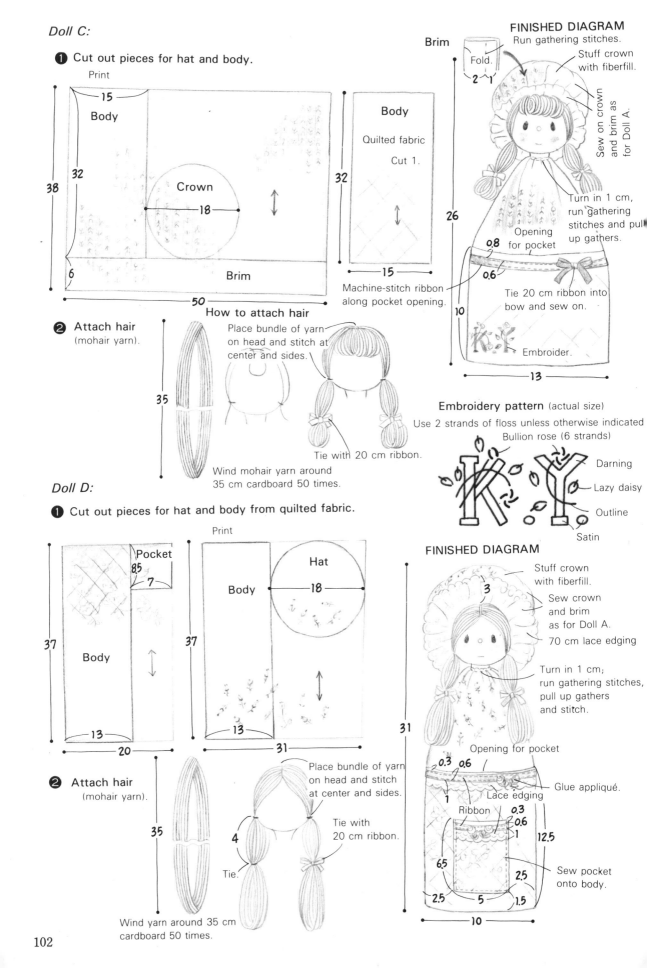

Doll E:

❶ Attach head to bodice.

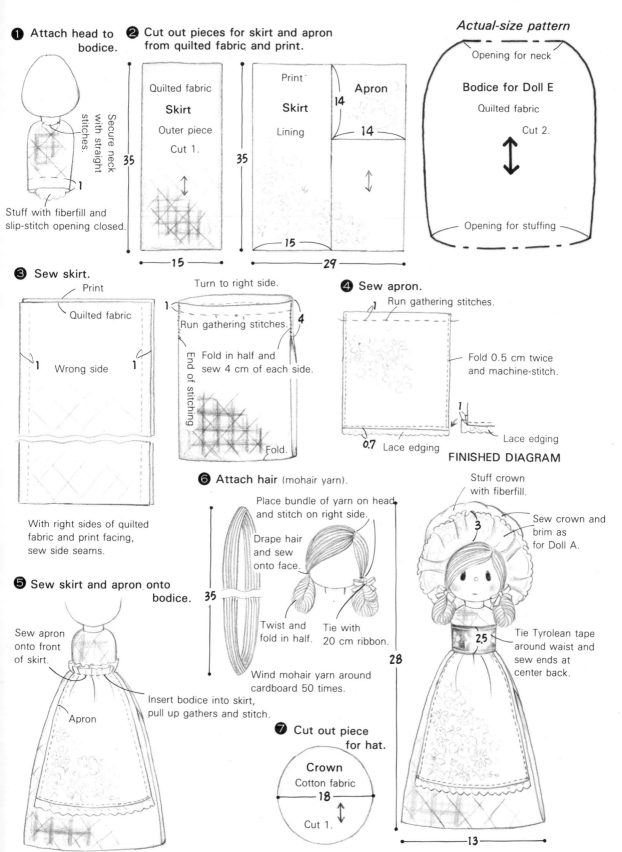

Secure neck with straight stitches.

Stuff with fiberfill and slip-stitch opening closed.

35

1

❷ Cut out pieces for skirt and apron from quilted fabric and print.

Quilted fabric

Skirt

Outer piece

Cut 1.

35

15

Print

Skirt

Lining

Apron

14

14

35

15

29

Actual-size pattern

Opening for neck

Bodice for Doll E

Quilted fabric

Cut 2.

Opening for stuffing

❸ Sew skirt.

Print

Quilted fabric

Wrong side

1

1

With right sides of quilted fabric and print facing, sew side seams.

Turn to right side.

1

Run gathering stitches.

End of stitching

Fold in half and sew 4 cm of each side.

4

Fold.

❹ Sew apron.

Run gathering stitches.

1

Fold 0.5 cm twice and machine-stitch.

1

Lace edging

0.7 Lace edging

FINISHED DIAGRAM

Stuff crown with fiberfill.

3

Sew crown and brim as for Doll A.

2.5

Tie Tyrolean tape around waist and sew ends at center back.

28

13

❺ Sew skirt and apron onto bodice.

Sew apron onto front of skirt.

Apron

Insert bodice into skirt, pull up gathers and stitch.

❻ Attach hair (mohair yarn).

Place bundle of yarn on head and stitch on right side.

Drape hair and sew onto face.

35

Twist and fold in half.

Tie with 20 cm ribbon.

Wind mohair yarn around cardboard 50 times.

❼ Cut out piece for hat.

Crown

Cotton fabric

18

Cut 1.

Helpful Kiddies, shown on pages 12 & 13.

MATERIALS:
For face: See page 69.
[For each doll] 4-ply yarn for hair.
[For A] Quilted fabric, 15 cm by 46 cm; denim, 28 cm by 46 cm; 2 emblems.
[For B] Cotton stripes, 20 cm by 40 cm; denim, 32 cm by 40 cm; one emblem; navy-colored wire #20.
[For C] Gingham checks, 10 cm by 30 cm; denim, 27 cm by 30 cm; 5 pencil-shaped buttons.
[For D] Cotton checks, 21 cm by 59 cm; denim, 24 cm by 44 cm; 2 emblems, 2 buttons, 1 cm in diameter.

FINISHED SIZE: See diagrams.
DIRECTIONS:
Make face following instructions on page 69–73.
For A: Make body and attach head to body. Sew curls all over head, make features, and put on cap.
For B, C, and D: Make as for A following individual instructions.

Actual-size patterns

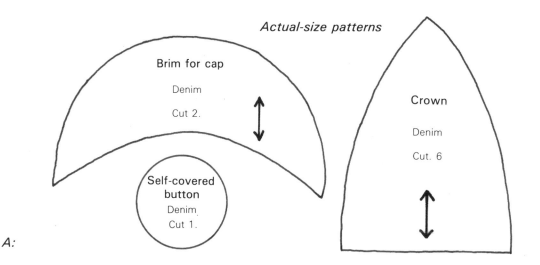

A:

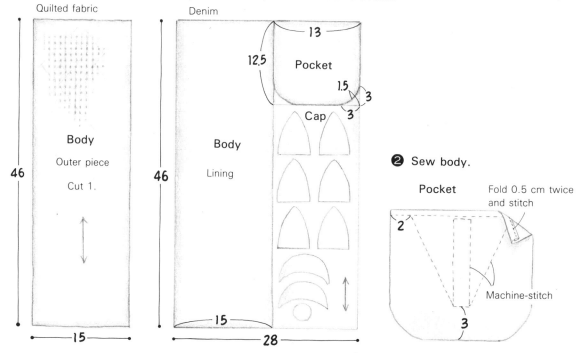

❶ Cut out pieces for body and pocket from quilted fabric and denim.

❷ Sew body.

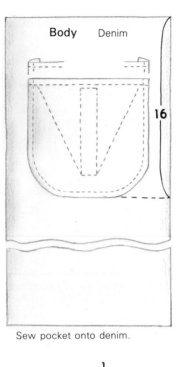

Body Denim

16

Sew pocket onto denim.

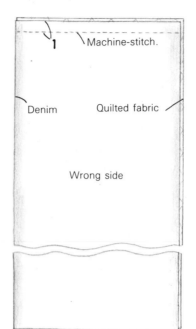

Machine-stitch.

1

Denim

Quilted fabric

Wrong side

With right sides of denim and quilted fabric facing, stitch top edges.

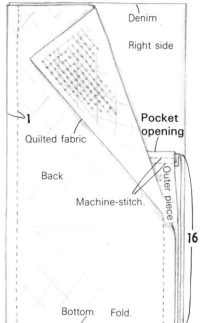

Denim

Right side

1

Quilted fabric

Pocket opening

Back

Outer piece

Machine-stitch.

16

Bottom Fold.

Machine-stitch twice along pocket opening. Fold under 16 cm and sew side seams.

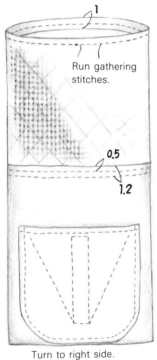

1

Run gathering stitches.

0.5

1.2

Turn to right side.

❸ **Insert neck into bag and stitch.**

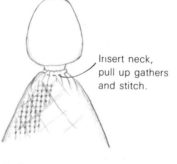

Insert neck, pull up gathers and stitch.

❹ **Attach hair** (bulky yarn).

Curls

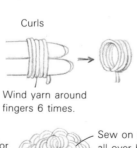

Wind yarn around fingers 6 times.

❺ **Make cap.**

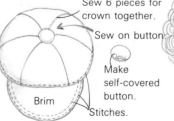

Sew 6 pieces for crown together.

Sew on button.

Make self-covered button.

Brim

Stitches.

Sew on curls all over head.

Nose

0.6

Eye

0.7

0.4

Glue nose and eyes onto face.

FINISHED DIAGRAM

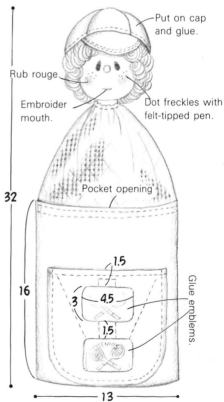

Put on cap and glue.

Rub rouge.

Embroider mouth.

Dot freckles with felt-tipped pen.

Pocket opening

32

16

1.5

3

4.5

1.5

Glue emblems.

13

105

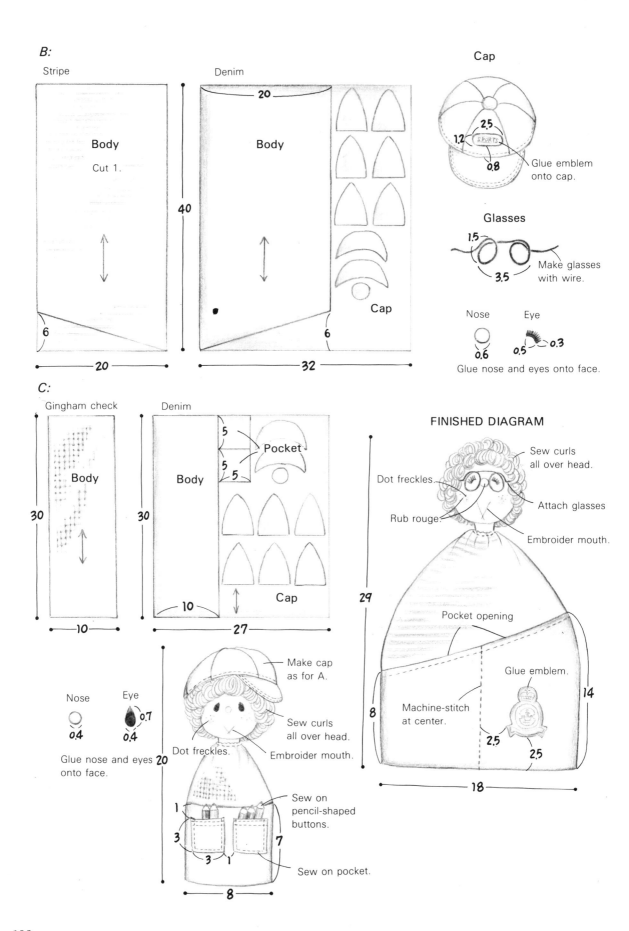

B:

Stripe

Body

Cut 1.

40

6

20

Denim

Body

20

6

Cap

Cap

2.5

1.2

SPORTS

0.8

Glue emblem onto cap.

32

Glasses

1.5

3.5

Make glasses with wire.

Nose

0.6

Eye

0.5 0.3

Glue nose and eyes onto face.

C:

Gingham check

Body

30

10

Denim

Body

30

5

5 5

Pocket

Cap

10

27

Nose

0.4

Eye

0.7

0.4

Glue nose and eyes onto face.

20

Make cap as for A.

Sew curls all over head.

Embroider mouth.

Dot freckles.

1

3

3 1

7

Sew on pencil-shaped buttons.

Sew on pocket.

8

FINISHED DIAGRAM

Sew curls all over head.

Dot freckles.

Rub rouge.

Attach glasses

Embroider mouth.

29

Pocket opening

8

Machine-stitch at center.

Glue emblem.

14

2.5

2.5

18

D:

① Cut out pieces for body.

Check

6

Body
Ⓐ
7
9.5

7
Ⓐ
6
9.5

9

Body

59

10

Bottom

29.5

6

12

21

Denim

6

Body

10

Bottom

44

6

24

22

Cap

② Sew body.

1

1

Join pieces A and B together.

4.5

Machine-stitch at center.

Bottom

Turn seam toward bottom.

4.5

Join pieces A and B together.

③ Attach neck to body.

Place front on back and pull up gathers.

Insert neck into back body.

Front

Check

Check

Wrong side

Denim

With right sides of A, B, and C facing, sew side seams.

Turn in 1 cm and run gathering stitches.

Turn in 1 cm and run gathering stitches.

7.5

21

Fold.

Turn to right side and fold in half.

Nose   Eye

0.3

0.4   0.5

Make cap as for A.

Glue nose and eyes onto face.

Sew curls all over head.

Dot freckles.

Embroider mouth

FINISHED DIAGRAM

Sew buttons onto front and back.

35

10

Glue emblems.

3   2.5

1

SPORTS   SPORTS

10

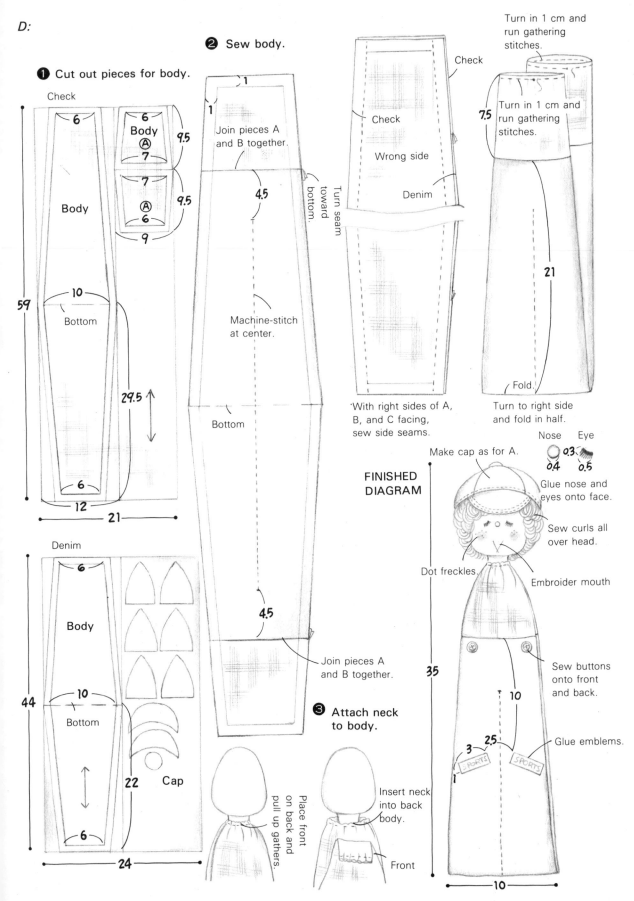

Actual-size patterns for Clowns, shown on pages 30 & 31.

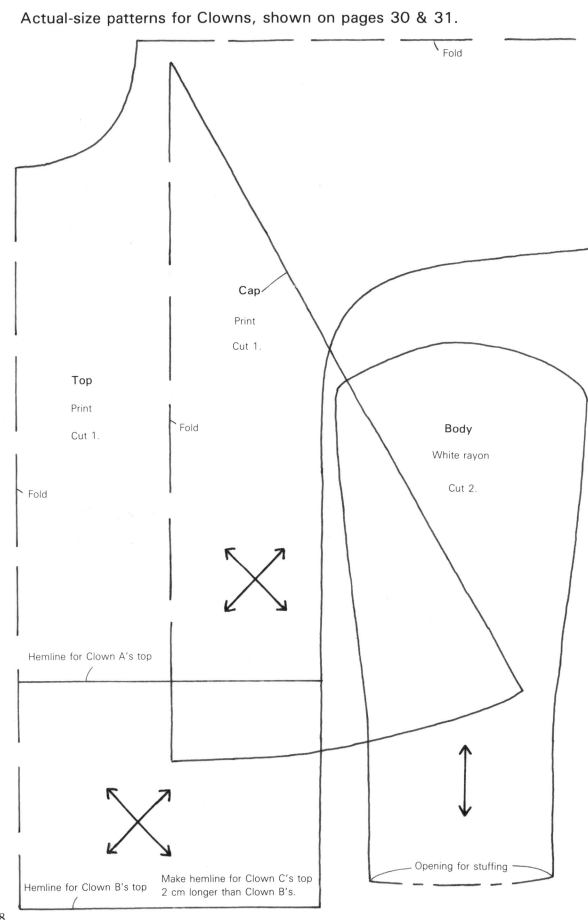

Fold

Cap

Print

Cut 1.

Top

Print

Cut 1.

Fold

Fold

Body

White rayon

Cut 2.

Hemline for Clown A's top

Hemline for Clown B's top

Make hemline for Clown C's top
2 cm longer than Clown B's.

Opening for stuffing

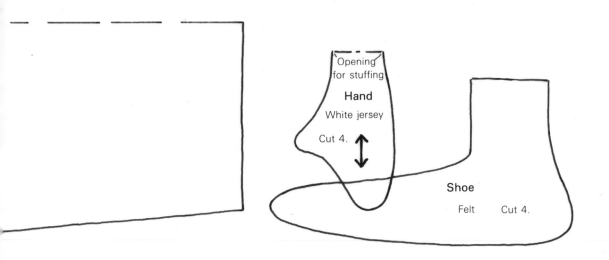

Opening
for stuffing

Hand

White jersey

Cut 4.

Shoe

Felt   Cut 4.

Actual-size patterns for Grandma and Twins, shown on pages 18 & 19.

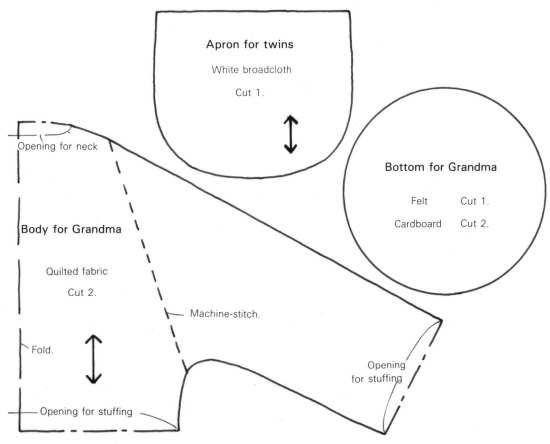

Apron for twins

White broadcloth

Cut 1.

Bottom for Grandma

Felt   Cut 1.

Cardboard   Cut 2.

Opening for neck

Body for Grandma

Quilted fabric

Cut 2.

Machine-stitch.

Fold.

Opening
for stuffing

Opening for stuffing

Message from the author

I feel like placing my hand made dolls here and there in my house instead of confining them in the doll case. If they were sitting by the pillows on the sofa or standing on the jam-bottles, I think they would create a warm and comfortable atmosphere around them. Because each doll is made with great care and all of them are so lovely and charming. I have been dreaming of living with dolls for a long time, but at the present it is impossible for me to do so. Do you know why? It is because I have a naughty kitten who likes to play with dolls very much. I have to keep all of the dolls in my room to protect them from this kitten. I must wait until he will be old enough to behave.

I do hope you will enjoy your life with dolls.

Last of all, I wish to thank the many people who have helped me publish this book from the bottom of my heart.

Kyoko Yoneyama